MEN'S LIB

Advance Praise for

Men's Lib and other Literary, Cultural and Personal Essays

Here is a collection of essays that strikes a balance between academicism and accessibility, a rare feat these days. The thematic range of these pieces written over fifteen years is amazing: from the idea of the nation to post-Colonialism, from feminism to translation theory, and from communalism to Negritude, subjects that are still topical and discussed by scholars and readers alike. There are personal essays that give the book an autobiographical tinge, and there are critical essays on acclaimed writers in Hindi and English like Nagarjun, Mangalesh Dabral, Nissim Ezekiel, and Dom Moraes. A fascinating collection in simple prose.

—Prof. K SATCHIDANANDAN, Eminent Poet-Critic
and Former Secretary, Sahitya Akademi
(India's National Academy of Letters)

Mr. Kumar Vikram presents here his views on a number of contemporary and important issues, in great writing. Deep dives into his topics open up new worlds, and for foreigners, many of the essays are perfect to get a better understanding of today's India. I was also quite impressed with his personal essays.

—CLAUDIA KAISER, International Publishing Maestro
and Vice-President, Frankfurt Book Fair

The provocative titling: MEN'S LIB is misleading. This eclectic collection of essays is a veritable smorgasbord of thought-provoking discussion by an erudite, decidedly empathetic male with vast-ranging knowledge across the socio-cultural and literary scape. Wedged between thin slices of some feminist questioning and whimsically personal takes lies very substantive scholarly material, handled with a deft easy touch. The rare insights in the textured inter-weave of the historical and literary in the two-part essay on Nation Building and the Dynamics of Translation alone justifies its purchase.

—RAMI CHHABRA, Celebrated Columnist
and Feminist Writer

Essays are landscapes incarnate and essayist a landscaper personified. This veritable collage of nineteen landscapes brings us face to face with a uniquely humane landscaper who draws upon time past and present, arrays of people then and now and places here and there to compose a rich complex of representations. In a broader context, he reconfigures contemporary history and its cultural icons, as he does larger social configurations, contested ideologies and literary canons. He takes us into multiple directions just as life takes us to and enables us to watch them from close quarters. As one moves from one landscape to another, one discovers one's own self in relation to this landscaper's affiliations and disaffiliations, as well as poetics and politics of life and letters. In this process one develops a camaraderie with him and discovers how personal meets with political, social with cultural and literary with bizarre. All of these are seen through the landscaper's progressive lenses that help us see things lying nearby and those at a remove with equal clarity. Developed over two decades, these landscapes richly mark the contours of our times at the far end of the last century and the inaugural decades of the present one.

—Prof. ANISUR RAHMAN
Eminent Poet, Translator and critic
Formerly Professor of English at Jamia Millia Islamia, New Delhi.

This is a work blazing with the spirit of a deep and large hearted humanism. The concerns of the book—political, literary and personal—are about catching a moving force that is at once iconoclastic and integrative. It stands firmly against provocative outbursts and finality of convictions. Bridges are rather built by appreciating the unresolved contours of living relationalities. Every single essay testifies to the fact that it is essential to mediate our convictions and sense of injustice through evolving and reflective intellectual processes. We can hear a rare adult voice which at once accepts life's finitude and yet celebrates the fundamental spirit of curiosity. In a world of bad faith and confusion, they give us some solid directions. The empathetic reader shall appreciate the enormous wisdom and rich aesthetic sensibility of a rooted internationalist.

—Prof. PRASANTA CHAKRAVARTY, Eminent Poet-Critic, Translator and Professor of English, University of Delhi

The genre of general essay has been in decline for some time. The laid back figure of the essayist, as a curious onlooker, interested citizen, impromptu thinker and 'unauthorised' but cautious interpreter of socio-cultural phenomena, too seems to have taken a back seat. But that is where the genre thrives most. The friendly form is most accommodative of the diverse themes, issues and contingent matters as they come to one's mind, and is, therefore, most expressive of an author's personality.

Kumar Vikram's range of interests, sense of form and observational acuity makes this collection of socio-political, literary and personal essays a useful, enjoyable and quietly encouraging read.

—ASAD ZAIDI, Eminent Poet-Critic, Translator and Founder, Three Essays Collective

MEN'S LIB

and other literary, cultural and personal essays

KUMAR VIKRAM

NIRALA

Nirala Publications
4637/20, Third Floor, Unit No 310,
Hari Sadan, Ansari Road, Daryaganj,
New Delhi 110002 India
niralabooks@yahoo.co.in
niralapublications.com

First Edition 2023

ISBN 978-81-9519-153-6 (Paperback)

ISBN 978-81-957816-2-1 (Hardcover)

Cover Design: Graphical House

Typeset at Ideal Publishing Solutions, New Delhi, India and
Printed at Chaman Enterprises, New Delhi

Dedications

To father
Late Prof Arun Kumar Sinha
(1940–2011)
for inculcating that spirit of enquiry and empathy

To mother
Mrs. Kamla Sinha
for inculcating that spirit of investing in relationships without any expectations

To Bhaiya
Shri Kumar Vivek
(1967–1997)
for initiating me into the world of literature and innovation

To Didi
Mrs Vatsala Sinha
For that understated warmth of protection since childhood

To Deepti
Friend and Life-partner
For being always there as a pillar of unquestioning support

"The man who finds his homeland sweet is still a tender beginner; he to whom every soil is as his native one is already strong; but he is perfect to whom the entire world is as a foreign land. The tender soul has fixed his love on one spot in the world; the strong man has extended his love to all places; the perfect man has extinguished his. From boyhood I have dwelt on foreign soil and I know with what grief sometimes the mind takes leave of the narrow hearth of a peasant's hut, and I know too how frankly it afterwards disdains marble firesides and panelled halls."

— **Hugh of Saint Victor** (c. 1096-1141), *The Didascalicon of Hugh of Saint Victor: A Medieval Guide to the Arts*, Book III, Chapter 19, p.101 (Translated from the Latin with an Introduction and Notes by Jerome Taylor; Columbia University Press, New York and London, 1961)

CONTENTS

LITERARY ESSAYS

PERSONAL ESSAYS

PREFACE

The essays of this volume were written and published on various platforms, including the author's blog, over a period of 15 years, between 2004-2020, to be precise. However, all of them have been thoroughly read and edited for this volume coming out in 2022. The 'Introduction' got written over the last six months or so. As one read through these essays for the reader of the post-Covid era, one was struck to note that despite the global Pandemic afflicting the world for more than two years, the core issues of human societies remain the same—whether it is the gender discourse or the politics of representation employed by various dominant communities, or whether it is the challenges posed by competing ideologies and identities. In fact, there is a greater degree of 'culture of complain' that permeate our day-to-day life.

These essays try to walk through various lanes and by-lanes of ideas and personalities believing them all to be part and parcel of one big village, or may be an apartment, which are interconnected, have corridors and lifts to link them, but due to biases and prejudices, one remains oblivious of the same. May be, this volume will become some kind of catalyst to open up new windows of dialogue and understanding in its own gentle way.

I take this opportunity to thank the Editor and Publisher of Nirala Publishers, Mr. Yuyutsu Sharma, an eminent poet and patron of poetry, for finding it fit to publish this volume there by fulfilling my long-held desire to see them in a book form.

I would also like to thank and acknowledge Spectrum Books, Sahitya Akademi, All India Radio, Indira Gandhi National Open University, New Delhi, *Academia.edu* from which platforms some of the essays included in this book appeared first over a period of time.

New Delhi
1 July 2022

Kumar Vikram

INTRODUCTION

'All Images are man-made'

It was in the year 2009 that I had an opportunity to visit London for the first time on an official tour to attend the London Book Fair in the month of April. During the visit, a tour of the city of London on the last day was part of the itinerary. London as a city seemed quite affable, mostly due to its architecture which related it to some of our cities like Delhi, Mumbai or Kolkata. It was so very easy to negotiate its metro trains or hail a cab unlike some other cities of Europe where language becomes a barrier. So one could read the signages, talk to pedestrians to seek directions, purchase water bottles or London underground tickets, and so on and so forth with lot of ease. English language connected us so very smoothly.

The comfort level that the city offered to me was surely due to the long underlying relationship that I as an Indian unconsciously and consciously shared with it due to the 'colonial' past. I believe that there was a sense of *déjà vu* or an unexplained familiarity also because as a student of English Literature one had numerous times sort of already travelled through the lanes and by-lanes of the city from *The Canterbury Tales* to Shakespeare's characters narrating their poetic woes at the city's Globe Theatre through the literary repartees played out in the bars and taverns of the city by Samuel

Johnson, Dryden and contemporaries to Wordsworth's *Westminster Bridge* to the demeaning and dehumanizing impact of the city on Oliver Twists of the novels of Dickens or the iconic Sherlock Holmes to Eliot's Prufrock *et al* loitering with them all on perhaps Baker Street or Oxford Street or Hyde Park!

A visit to The National Gallery located at the Trafalgar Square was on the top of the agenda. I quite keenly looked forward to seeing in person original works of art of European Renaissance and Modern masters like Michelangelo, Leonardo da Vinci, Raphael, Anthony van Dyck, Rembrandt, Vincent van Gogh, Pablo Picasso—the names that one had lived with as a student of literature.

Things were moving on quite well, before, right at the centre of Trafalgar Square, a prominent and imposing statue of Henry Havelock (1795-1857), the British general who is particularly associated with India and his recapture of Cawnpore (now Kanpur) and Lucknow during India's First War of Independence in 1857 (named as Sepoy's Mutiny by the British historians), hit me like a bolt from the colonial past. The description of the statue eulogising someone, who is known as one of the foremost generals who led the repression and killings of Indian revolutionaries, was all the more disturbing for me. It went something like this:

> *To Major General Sir Henry Havelock KCB and his brave companions in arms during the campaign in India 1857.*
>
> *"Soldiers! Your labours, your privations, your sufferings and your valour, will not be forgotten by a grateful country." H. Havelock*

Having been an independent researcher as well as a publishing editor with deep interest in post-colonial and feminist studies, one has been exposed to various layers and competing ideas about nationalism and national heroes, still that particular statue of Havelock with those words at the Trafalgar Square which I discovered that day[1] drove home so very pithily the costs of the 'comfort level' that London as a city offered to me during that visit. The comfort level was nothing but a by-product of the historical discomfort and discrimination that allowed me to feel it that way.

But, 75 years down the line since India's independence and that of many other colonized nations of Asia, Africa and Latin America, the post-colonial milieu is no longer that linear—that of the hero of the colonial powers being a villain in the colonised world. Post-Cold War, Post-Globalization, and also Post-Internet world, have thrown up new narratives in both sides of the Colonial divide as well as within those divides, made even sharper due to the emerging Feminist, Black and other Identity-based movements, such as those by the Dalits and other marginalized communities in India.

Let us take forward the complex 'legacy' of Havelock to understand these nuances as a test case to make out how the socio-political and cultural world order has been undergoing subtle and not-so-subtle changes. First, it needs to be mentioned here that there are some other statues (including at Mowbray Park, Sunderland) and public parks named after Havelock in England (and also in Singapore and New Zealand) to cherish his role as the 'hero' of his 'campaigns' in British India. But as history would have it, his tomb at Lucknow (visited by Prince of Wales in 1911) made by his wife and family still stands in Chander Nagar, Alambagh area of Lucknow, Uttar Pradesh. The following verses are inscribed on his tomb, which came up upon his death in 1857:

> "His ashes in a peaceful urn shall rest;
> His name a great example stands to show
> How strangely high endeavours may be blessed,
> When piety and valour jointly go."[2]

Havelock's tomb has survived in India till now having escaped any post-colonial revisionist gaze that has been the norm all over the world. It is also symbolic of the fact that the memories, traces and realities of more than 200 years of British Raj can hardly be erased physically because not only that would not be the best way to overcome colonial domination, but also because simply there are too many of them. Having said this, an Island named after him in the Andamans was renamed in December 2018 as Swaraj Island, as a tribute to one of the stalwarts of Indian independence, Netaji Subhas Chandra Bose. Bose had hoisted the Indian flag at Port Blair on 30 December 1943 and proclaimed the Andaman and Nicobar Islands as liberated from British rule. He had subsequently named Neill Island (named after another British Brigadier-General, James Neill, who had led the counter attack against Indian revolutionaries on behalf of British Raj in 1857) as Shaheed Island and Havelock Island as Swaraj Island.

The official renaming of Havelock islands must have been long overdue in India even though popularly they are still known and mentioned as Havelock islands only. But the 'legacy' of the 'hero' of British campaign in India becomes all the more complicated when we learn that in his own country questions have been raised about his 'contribution'. In the year 2000, a big uproar broke out when Ken Livingstone, who served as the Mayor of London from 2000 (the year the office of Mayor of London was created) till 2008, questioned the very rationale of having the statues of Havelock and Napier on the plinth at the Trafalgar Square, wondering "he did not know who the generals were or what they had done to deserve their prime positions alongside George IV and Nelson."[3]

Further underlining the spatial movement of time and history, a part of Havelock Road in Southall, London (known as 'Mini

India'), was renamed as 'Guru Nanak Road' in January 2021 by the Ealing Council with the Councillor Julian Bell, the leader of Ealing Council, saying:

> We need to make sure that our public realm, our statues, road names and buildings reflect our diversity, and not a frozen past where colonialism, racism and the slave trade were present and celebrated.[4]

The renaming of the road was also seen as part of the contemporary 'vote-bank politics' linked with Southhall, dominated by the immigrants from Indian sub-continent, with majority from Punjab in India.

However, since the colonial engagement is complicated hence the renaming started a debate of various hues: some 'progressive' British welcoming the move, while others mourning it as 'erasing British colonial history'; from the Indian side a part of the Southall population welcomed it for recognising the diversity of contemporary social life of England and applauded the removal of Major Havelock's name, asserting he was an 'oppressor' and 'colonial murderer'. Some Sikhs, however, questioned the plausibility of naming a road after the revered Guru Nanak, the founder of Sikhism, since no one had ever thought of naming a road after Jesus Christ or Prophet Mohammad. The enlightened few pointed out that many Sikh soldiers had actually fought under Major-General Havelock during 1857 uprisings in India against the British rule.

In order to further problematize the dynamics of this coloniser-colonised relationship in the contemporary times, one would do well to remember and refer to Neill Statue Satyagrah undertaken in 1927 itself at Madras (now Chennai) by the nationalist leaders demanding the removal of the statue of Brigadier-General James Neill (1810-1857)[5]– the second-in-command of Henry Havelock at Benaras, Allahabad and Lucknow– situated at Mount Road (now Anna Salai) since he was identified as 'butcher of Allahabad' during 1857 uprising. James Neill, who was serving as Colonel in the first European Regiment of East India Company at Madras called "Madras Fusiliers", was sent to Benaras in June 1857 on way to Kanpur with his regiment as a reinforcement force. He achieved notoriety for ordering massacres of not only Indian revolutionaries at Benares and later at Allahabad and Lucknow but also of commoners to infuse the sense of acute fear of the British Raj that had been challenged by the revolutionaries.

A significant work on 1857 revolution, edited by Pramod K Nayar, reproduces an extract from James Neill's letter as quoted in *History of Sepoy War in India* by John Kaye[6], which provides an insight into the most inhuman *modus operandi* adopted by James Neill to avenge the killing of British officers, and men and women by the revolutionaries:

> Every stain of that innocent blood [British] shall be cleared up and wiped out, previous to their execution, by such miscreants as may be hereafter apprehended, who took an active part in mutiny…and the Provost-Marshall will use the lash in forcing anyone objecting to complete the task. After properly cleaning up his portion the culprit is to be immediately hanged, and for this purpose a gallows will be erected close at hand.[7]

In the 'Introduction' to the book, Nayar writes:

> Reinforcements for Kanpur, led by James Neill, had reached Benaras on 3 June, before the rising had taken place. Benaras became a spot of bother. Neill sought to disarm native soldiers and delayed moving to Allahabad as he hanged 'mutineers' at every conceivable opportunity. Mango trees, it was said, often had bodies hanging upon them. Neill arrived in Allahabad on 11 June…[8]

James Neil was killed in action and was shot in the head at Khas Bazaar, Lucknow on 25 September 1857.

Two statues, one at Madras in 1860, and the other at his birthplace, Wellington Square, Ayr, Ayrshire, Scotland, a year before in 1859, were put up with identical inscription on the pedestal of Neill's statue:

James George Smith Neill
A.D.C to the Queen
Lieut Colonel in the Madras Fusiliers
Brigadier General in India
A brave, resolute, self-reliant soldier
Universally acknowledged as the first
Who stemmed the torrent of rebellion in Bengal
He fell gloriously
At the relief of Lucknow
25th September 1857
Aged 47.[9]

James Neill's notoriety and cruelty must have been of meanest possible level as a full-scale movement to remove his statue from the landscape of Madras became a major milestone in the anti-colonial resistance in Tamil Nadu, and India as such. The agitators came from all over the Madras Presidency and were led by S. N. Somayajulu of Tirunelveli. Several agitators were arrested and sentenced to prison terms ranging from a few weeks to a year of rigorous imprisonment. After the major leaders – Somayajulu and Swaminatha Mudaliar – were arrested, K. Kamaraj became the leader of the agitation. As this document notes:

> The Tamilnadu Volunteer Corps, an independent body of local inhabitants, spearheaded the movement for the removal of the statue. When Gandhiji toured Madras in the first week of September 1927

> he lent his support to the volunteers to continue the movement on the condition that the movement should conform to the conditions for a proper satyagraha and that the movement should be independent and self-supporting.[10]

In fact, Mahatma Gandhi had very close engagement with the movement leaders, and this particular excerpt from *Young India* shows how he could turn the question of removal of the statue something into a test of colonial resistance—as a carrier of his larger goal to train and turn the freedom seekers from the statue into freedom seekers of the enslaved country.

> What we have to deal with is the statue and not even the statue as such. We seek to destroy the principle for which the statue stands. We wish to injure no man. And we wish to gain our object by enlisting public opinion not excluding English opinion in our favour by self-suffering. Here there is no room for the language of anger and hate.
>
> Agitation for the removal of the statue is agitation for the removal of but a symptom of a grave disease. And while the removal of the statue will not cure the disease it will alleviate the agony and point the way to reaching the disease itself. It is also often possible to reach a deep-seated disease by dealing with some of its symptoms.[11]

In the Madras Legislative Council, thirteen notices were given to pass a Resolution for the removal of the Neill's statue. Eventually the statue was removed through a Corporation Resolution in 1937, during the first Congress ministry, and is now placed in the Madras Museum.[12]

In order to understand the rather piquant cycle of time as already noted in the case of the legacy of Havelock, one can find a petition going on for the last two years on change.org put out by the representatives of the small Indian community at Aye[13] for removal of Neill statue, on the one hand, and a similar suggestion given by a native Aye blogger, Francesco Bonfanti, with his sentiments stemming from

> The murder of George Floyd under the knee of a white American police officer (that) sparked global outrage and has led to wider questions of the legacy of colonialism, slavery and continuing systemic racism against Black communities around the world.[14]

This train of events presented here to highlight the saga of image-making and iconoclasm—literally as well as figuratively—with its Indian linkages is actually just a drop out of the ocean of global anti-racist and anti-colonial counter to claim public space and erase memory of the oppressors in the post-colonial milieu. As Enzo Traverso, Italian scholar of European intellectual history, so very succinctly records in an article written for an Indian journal:

> Anti-racism is a battle for memory...Everywhere, anti-racist movements have put the past into question by targeting monuments that symbolise the legacy of slavery and colonialism: the Confederate general Robert E. Lee in Virginia; Theodore Roosevelt in New York City; Christopher Columbus in many US cities; the Belgian king Leopold II in Brussels; the slave trader Edward Colston in Bristol; Jean-Baptiste Colbert, Finance Minister for Louis XIV and author of the infamous Code Noir in France; the father of modern Italian journalism and former propagandist for fascist colonialism, Indro Montanelli, and so on.[15]

But the question arises if the targeting of memory and monuments associated with previous oppressors enough? It is so because ultimately the test for the leaders/forces at the helm of the decolonization is to provide a counter narrative to bring concrete change on the economic and socio-political plains. Of all the anti-colonial resistance leaders, Mahatma Gandhi was a rare example of someone who could keep the negative emotions—hatred and violence—in check and seek to look at actions from a moral standpoint as well. His approach during the Neill Satyagrah Movement, as already mentioned, provides a prototype before the forces behind decolonization, and is worth reproducing once again:

> What we have to deal with is the statue and not even the statue as such. We seek to destroy the principle for which the statue stands.

Naturally, this kind of idea of colonial resistance does not pretend itself to be frozen in time. Rather it has the wherewithal to understand the complexities and challenges of post-colonial milieu which demand as well as push us to respond in an integrative manner keeping the unresolved contours of gender, sexuality, religion, caste, race, ethnicity, language etc. in mind.

Understandably, due to the conscious as well as unconscious evasion of the moral or ethical aspects of the 'unresolved contours' or 'fault lines' of decolonization, the same has come under some insightful critique with the gaze now being slightly moving towards those at the helm of the decolonization process in the previously colonized world, more so, because ironically many of them landed up under dictatorship. Albert Memmi (1920-2020), the distinguished French-Tunisian writer and a theorist of decolonization, finding it 'necessary to satirize certain taboos', stated:

> Like the colonized, the decolonized is not a saint: how could he be and continue to live through such an agitated period of his history?[16]

Then, in a scathing attack on the perpetuation of the image-making of the 'new rulers', he makes observations that lay bare the entire question of dismantling of statues of the previous rulers without any moralistic dimensions and more as evasion of the challenges of nation building that confront them:

> The statues of former leaders that dotted the cities of the past appear old-fashioned compared to the modern reproductions in stone, bronze, or oils of the new world leader...In this systematic enterprise of seduction, television is a providential tool...A day doesn't go by when he doesn't show up in everyone's living room, not, as in days gone by, in some stylised portrait hung on the wall, but presiding over a meeting, opening a clinic or religious building, commemorating a national event—present, past, or future. A handful of signs of his prestige, light fixtures along the central avenue, a few megalomaniacal monuments, grandiose but questionable projects, help eradicate the memory of the mud in the streets, the piles of garbage, and the absence of a working sewage system.[17]

In his *Culture and Imperialism* (1994), Edward Said had referred to Albert Memmi as one of the few intellectuals who could bridge the gap between 'the coloniser and the colonised' and his fatigue and desperation with the derailment of the dream of actual decolonization in some of the previously colonised states needs to be looked at seriously, even though with some pinch of salt.

***

To take the symbolism of the politics of replacement of statues or renaming of roads and monuments further as a symbol of the assertion as well as 'correction' of national identities in the post-colonial world, we would get a new dimension if we analyze that rarely do we see a statue of a male personality getting replaced with the statue of a female personality and so on and so forth. It is simply because the narratives of national reconstruction fought shy of placing gender balance as the key priority area—both in policy and in practice. In fact, even the statues and images made of women suffer from, what John Berger in his landmark book *Ways of Seeing*[18] terms, 'male gaze'. Rather, when Berger underlines 'all images are man-made', one wonders the scale of dismantling of images/statues that would require on part of the women folk taking men as their oppressors and colonisers down the ages. Two focal essays of this collection—the lead essay 'Men's Lib' and the second lead on 'Taj Mahal'—take up this issue, though the approach and treatment of these essays may not be falling strictly under the conventional 'feminist' discourse. In fact, even their unconventionality can be questioned.

For example, the concept of 'Men's Liberation' is not that new and in the context of the American society, one may view it with an attitude of 'been-there, done-that'. After all, it was way back in 1970s itself that Jack Nicolas wrote his book *Men's Liberation: A New Definition of Masculinity*[19] questioning the myths that have gone into the making of the gender role of men and their masculinity and how they impact the man-woman relationship. This is also well-documented how the Men's liberation movement later got split into many other contradictory and ideologically not-so-clear movements such as the self-defeating 'Men's rights movement'.

But in the 21st Century India, 'Men's Lib' is an idea that needs to be brought back to the centre stage of popular discourse because it is something that has not been discussed as a structured concept in academic or general social thought process in our country. Even after 75 years of Indian independence, we find patriarchal ideas and notions defining the socio-cultural and political dynamics with masculine and feudal narrative trying to objectify and control the choices of women—and men alike, by default. The lead essay thus tries to put the gaze on men themselves and how they need to be rescued from the notions of masculinity not really created by the contemporary men but being with them as a *fait accompli* so that they can respond to women and gender-equality issues in a natural manner, rather than being arrogant or with false notions of superiority complex.

As this Introduction gets finalised, one hears the stunning news of the reversal of legal abortion rights by the Supreme Court of USA which were granted to women there after long years of debate and struggle in 1970s itself. The disturbing nature of this regressive development should not only make a common American man, but men all across the globe, introspect at the extent of control the 'male-infrastructure' has and still wants to have over women's rights. It may be the right time for men to get liberated out of these sickening and cumbersome self-inflicted gender codes and exit the gender-equality discourse as a coloniser and start participating in its meaningful decolonization. All this may (and, in fact, does) sound too Utopian but as a character, Luciente, in the pathbreaking novel titled, *Women on the Edge of Time*, of the noted contemporary American 'Utopian' novelist and feminist, Marge Piercy, stated, we can only hope to bear the fruits of the seeds in reality that we sow in our imagination:

> We can quarrel joyously with each other about important matters of idea and art. The vestiges of old ways will fade. I can't know that time—any more than you can ultimately know us. We can only know what we can truly imagine. Finally what we see comes from ourselves.[20]

Incidentally, this character called Luciente in the novel is an androgynous young woman who is time-traveling from a future (the date is given as 2137), in which a spectrum of goals of the political and social agenda of the late sixties' and early seventies' radical movements have been realised. This is indicative of the fact that in our imagination also we do factor in the snakes and ladders route that we have to take in attaining equality in all spheres hence realising that the path will not only be circuitous but also criss-cross each other to undo many achievements that are taken for granted.

***

The essays* of this volume not only express but actually emerge from the fault lines of the pre-colonial and post-colonial discourse in India and elsewhere which dominate our day-to-day discourse in public as well as private spaces. As a matter of fact, how the public discourse impacts the private and the personal space which in turn impinges upon the wider universal debates may be considered as the guiding force of the explorations that some of these essays try to make. Hence from a long essay delving into the role of translation and interpretation in the context of nation-building to essays on the aspects of 'reading' culture, some contemporary poets, and family 'heroes'—all get joined in one way or the other and hope to take along the reader as well in this exploration further. In this context, the perspective offered by the 12th century German mystic settled in France, Hugh of St. Victor, as quoted in the Epigraph to this book, would keep us in good stead since it throws before us a demanding intellectual objectivity to look at the emerging ideas and issues.

***

**For the sake of 'neatness' on the cover, to put it frankly, only the term 'cultural' has been used . However, one would surely like to call them 'socio-cultural' essays– because that is what they are– as they appear inside the book on the 'contents' page and the first section break.*

SOCIO-CULTURAL ESSAYS

CHAPTER 1

FEMALE FOETICIDES AND LIMITATIONS OF FEMINISM

Can MEN'S LIB Provide the Answer?

When the 2001 Census brought to the fore the horrifying fact of depleting sex ratio due to the large scale female foeticide and infanticide in the country, one could not but reflect upon and get disturbed at the civilizational collapse that it depicted. The 2011 census only reinforced the depleting sex-ratio due to the continued inhuman practice of female foeticide and infanticide. As per the Census 2011, the total sex ratio in India was 940 per 1000 males and the child sex ratio (children in the age group of 0–6) is 914 girl children per every 1000 boy children. Though, statistically, the overall female sex ratio increased by 0.75 % in the Census 2011 as compared to the previous Census of 2001, an analysis at micro levels has shown trends which are quite disturbing. A *Lancet* study published in 2022 that looked at the trends in missing females at birth in India from 1981 to 2016 found out that 'between the 2001 and 2011 censuses, sex selective abortions appeared to have increased in nearly three-quarters of India's districts (small administrative areas, each with about 2 million people).[1]

While traditionally the so-called 'women-hating' badlands of the North India like Haryana (877 girl children per every 1000 boy children), the national capital of Delhi (866: 1000), Chandigarh (818: 1000), Punjab (893) have been in the forefront of this reverse sex-ratio trend, the problem seems to have become all the more alarming if the child sex ratio is seen closely which is faring even worse not only in these states of the North, but also in the 'women-friendly' states like Kerala and Tamil Nadu. During this one decade, while the child sex-ratio has fallen down sharply in states like Punjab (from 961: 1000 to 846: 1000) and Haryana (from 954 to 830), the states like Kerala (from 965 to 959) and Tamil Nadu (from 959 to 946) have also shown a downward trend with some of the districts of these states showing much lesser average than the state average. The situation becomes all the more horrible when we are told that the trend is far stronger in urban rather than rural areas, and among the literates rather than the illiterates. In this light, the disturbing trend of Kerala with its highest literacy rate in the country can be cited. Underlining this, a *Times of India* report stated:[2]

> Kerala's unique sex ratio - 52% females to 48% males - is under threat from an 'invisible' quarter: the state's increasingly skewed child sex ratio. In both the 2001 and 2011 census, there has been a significant decrease in the number of girls compared to boys in the 0–6 age category. State health department statistics reveal that the child sex ratio has fallen in nine out of 14 districts in the past ten years. While the average number of girl children (the child sex

ratio is calculated per 1,000 boys) in the state decreased from 963 to 959, it is the disparate district-wise figures that are troubling.

This report only re-emphasised what an *Economic and Political Weekly* commentary had underlined following the 2001 census.[3] In fact, at the national level, child sex-ratio has been decreasing in every census (from 983 in 1951 to 914 in 2011), the period during which literacy rate has increased from nearly 15% to 74%. The depleting child sex-ratio is of greater concern because it is generally believed that if a girl child can survive till the age of six or so, her chances of surviving are much brighter. Hence infanticide, which is many a time prolicide/filicide, seems to be becoming a bigger monster making murderers out of the so-called parents and guardians. The smugness with which we have come to accept that spread of education and economic growth can correct gender bias becomes all too evident here.

Men's Lib, an 'offspring' of Feminism

The 'obsession for son' as sanctified by the Hindu faith as well as deeply entrenched socio-cultural customs permeating other faiths and girl child as a financial liability due to age-old custom of dowry prevalent in all religious-social communities in one form or the other are the twin reasons that bring out the devil in our societal attitude as expressed through female foeticide and infanticide. The hypocrisy in gender bias becomes all the more poignant when we find that despite these ground realities, the idea of women as 'powerful'—embodiment of *Shakti*—is very much a part and parcel of our patriarchal culture consecrated through religion.

What is most distressing is that the alarming imbalance in sex-ratio and pronounced social preference for son have stuck their roots despite the overall ambience of civil rights, gender equality, feminist ideas, wide-ranging constitutional reforms under which the educated and the progressive in India have been apparently brought up in the post-independence era. The question that rankles one is that has the women's liberation movement in the country failed to dent this deep-rooted gender prejudice that envelops our social psyche? Or has everything been left into the domain of the feminists, the women fighting for equal and dignified status for themselves in the society, making men passive partner in the longing for this change? One may ask that considering the deepness of this societal attitude, is the movement for women's liberation enough or something called the Men's Liberation Movement (Men's Lib, for short) as its natural 'offspring' too should come into play to correct the gender bias?

Men's Lib was perhaps first propounded by the American psychologist Joseph Pleck in the 1970s in the USA. Its basic premise is that while woman needs to be liberated from the clutches of man and his chauvinistic ideas, man as a social being also needs to be liberated from the gender prejudices that he has not built as an individual being but which have been handed down to him as something given, as some kind of universal and realised truth. Men's Lib, as a lateral extension of the feminist movement, has had its chequered history as an academic debate in the western social and intellectual discourses and it may be interesting to look at it from the Indian perspective in the contemporary context to underline the possibility of saving man from his ill-conceived notions of manhood with its deeply disturbing socio-political and cultural connotations.

It is also a more serious and more introspective response of men to the gender issues and to Feminism as an 'ism' in itself, as it tries to negotiate with the doubts expressed by male-feminists like Stephen Heath who believed that men entering into the discourses of feminism 'may be tempted to colonize it'. As Prof. Wes Chapman,

Associate Professor of English, Illinois Wesleyan University quotes Heath's following words from the latter's work 'Male Feminism':

> the point after all is that this a matter for women, that it is their voices and actions that must determine the change and redefinition. . . . Women are the subjects of feminism, its initiators, its makers, its force . . . Men are the objects, . . . agents of the structure to be transformed, . . . carriers of the patriarchal mode; and my desire to be a subject there too in feminism–to be a feminist—is then only the last feint in the long history of *their* colonisation.[4]

It is a kind of realisation that a mere adoption of a patronizing tone towards women's issues on the part of men may not take the cause of man-woman relationship much further and that a more concrete and more self-analytical response about the particular male attitudes to women is called for. The idea that manhood somehow depends on the subjugation of other people has hurt men too as the idea trains them consciously as well as unconsciously to oppress, to take upon themselves a hollow superiority complex and in turn to become brutal. Men's Lib underlines that it is this skewed male gender role inflicted upon the men as they grow up that stifles their development as a 'wholesome' human being.

Hence societal attitude towards man and woman seems to damage the male of the species even more fatally in some sense as this damage is neither recognized by the society nor by the individual, whereas in the case of women, the prejudiced societal attitude towards them is recognized, most certainly in theory and many a time in practice, by the society as well as the individual. As a result, while the talk of women getting liberated from male chauvinistic ideas gains currency, as it is understood because it is obvious, the mention of men themselves being in need of such a liberation has the propensity to be received on a plane contrary.

One may say that it is an inverted 'White Man's Burden', where the White Man, as a symbol of everything dominant, needs to get off his self-imposed burden ironically treasured by him as his whiteness. Thus Men's Lib seeks ways to liberate and disencumber man from his self-proclaimed burdens.

Steve Biddulph, an influential Australian author of books such as *Secret of Happy Children, Raising Boys,* and *The New Manhood*, activist, psychologist and one of the most eminent philosophers of Men's Lib, has been very emphatically able to underline how boys can be 'trained during the first two decades' of their life to develop into 'mature and loving men', while also stating 'that this process frequently does not take place'. In his article, 'How We Turn Boys Into Creeps',[5] Biddulph states

> Many men feel themselves, secretly, to be creeps; but only because they have been trapped in the inequality of gender relationships. Relating to others as human beings, on equal terms, entails the risk of rejection, the need for negotiation, all the incipient vulnerabilities of love. For a person who feels themself (sic) to be inferior or repulsive,this kind of intimacy is just too risky. The men who leer and wolf-whistle from building sites, for example, only ever do so from the safety of a group. (And gang rape is an extension of this pattern). One-to-one, these men lose all confidence — especially around an attractive or capable woman.

Further down in the article, Biddulph suggests "a men's movement/women's movement alliance" so that society as a whole can come upto comprehensive solutions to gender bias as expressed in our daily lives, representations in the media etc.

The socialization process of a boy getting groomed to become a man, thus, needs a paradigm shift. And more than learning new ways, the paradigm shift involves unlearning of centuries old prejudices and hollow gender elitism to overcome male anxiety of fitting in a particular social mould is quite akin to the feminist movement that empowers women to overcome the female anxiety to overcome prescribed gender roles. Hence it looks at the possibility of an alliance between men's movement and women's movement for a broader sensitizing of man-woman relationship.

The premises of Men's Lib also take some burden off the feminists who invariably took upon themselves the twin responsibility of walking together with men as well as reforming them, thereby granting men the role of a reactionary in the whole process. In fact, if one tries to look at the some of the earlier feminist writings, one realises that the feminists envisaged an equal role for men as a way to convince them of the intentions and benefits of feminism for them. But in practice it has resulted in dragging the men along without really looking at the socio-psychological anxieties and expectations that make up their persona. For example, we find that writing in the Sunday edition of *The Washington Post* (June 7, 1970, the 'International Year of Woman'), Gloria Steinem,[6] freelance contributor to *The New York Magazine* stated in her article "'Women's Liberation' Aims to Free Men, Too" and exhorted that the feminists "want to liberate men from... inhuman roles as well...and women's liberation is Men's Liberation too," because the feminists would like to share the work of men and expect them to reciprocate.

Perhaps this aspect, the aspect of Men's Lib, would have to be primarily negotiated by men themselves with the female of the species playing the much needed supportive role. The alliance between women's lib and men's lib would then have to be bridged by male-feminists on the one hand and female-men's lib advocates on the other. The possibilities of the latter brand would need to be worked out from the original feminist ideas with certain modifications thereby expanding the limiting scope of feminism as we understand it today. Thus, Men's Lib, by insisting on not turning our boys into arrogant and foetus-killing sons and sons-in-law through a process of unlearning, can take upon itself a more positive role in supplementing the effort to achieve man-woman equality so that men are not left repeating the Wordsworthian lament "What Man has made of Man."

Complexities of Men's Lib in India and Dalit/ Minorities/Tribal Discourses

However, in the Indian context the basic premises of Men's Lib need to be scrutinised. It is so because any movement worth its name must negotiate with the socio-political and cultural realities of its context. The biggest scepticism that Man's Lib movement in India would have to suffer may come in the form of the enquiries from the margins through Dalit/Minorities/Tribal discourses. The male of the species of these communities to begin with (not bringing in women of the marginalised communities at this stage whose concerns we will handle in the following paras), cannot but be justifiably concerned about the ways to handle the stereotyping and negative image-making of the people by the dominant/forward/ majority classes. These stereotypes since time immemorial create a different kind of complexity and anxiety, which may be divergent from the male of a dominant class. One may presume that a Dalit male would rather resist, revolt and assert his individual as well as community identity, rather than be obsessed with the anxiety to not fit in any prescribed gender role.

The genre of autobiography or autobiographical fiction that has been so effectively used by the writers from the marginalised communities to graphically narrate the inhuman practices, customs and brutalising that they have suffered since generations may not be in conformity with the kind of brutalising of male psyche that the Western psychologists as mentioned above may have in consideration. It is so, because the brutalising of the male psyche in the first case makes men feel inferior and inward looking, in the second case we are thinking of the misplaced superiority complex with which men grow up. In order to understand this, a small passage from the Dalit writer Mohandas Namishray's autobiographical Hindi work *Apne Apne Pinjarey* (which may be roughly translated as 'Our Own Isolated Cages'):

> We had been slaves since generations. The moment a mother bore a child, its caste would get imprinted on its forehead. It would be instantly made to realise its caste…Every now and then they would call us Chamatte and women as Chamatties. When they talked with each other they would contemptuously refer to us as that Chamatta, O Chamaari, What the hell, you Chamaar![7]

Instances of such name-calling and brutalising and far worse are more a rule and reality of life than being exceptions among the Dalit community which many other such autobiographies written across the country have been able to bring to the mainstream from the confines of the society's best kept secrets. Hence the premises of Men's Lib may appear to be at the odds with what the Dalits and other such marginalised communities have to experience.

Having said this, it may be instructive to quote the following para and then come to its context in order to explore as well as underline the feasibility and the possibilities of Men's Lib in the context of the experience of the marginalised communities:

> My husband was highly educated, a writer and a well- placed officer of the Government of India. He received a plaque and also pension

for being a freedom fighter. But my husband never respected me, rather due to daily physical fights and abuses, I was compelled to leave the house and move court. I spent forty years in that house. During the wrecked days of my life after leaving the house, my daughter Sujata supported me. While staying with my daughter, I could summon moral courage and resources to write…

The above para has been quoted by Mohandas Namishray from a Dalit woman's autobiography in his article published on *anaytha.com*, which is a painful narrative of the multiple colonialism that a dalit woman has to negotiate—of the upper caste male, upper caste female and dalit men, to specify a few. Dalit discourse has justifiably found a connect with the Black Movement of the USA, and it may be proper to quote a para from one of the earliest writings of one of the Black feminists, Mary Ann Weathers. In an article titled 'An Argument For Black Women's Liberation As A Revolutionary Force'[8] she wrote what may be termed as very enlightening in the context of man-woman liberation movements with race, and one should add in Indian context, caste, minorities and tribes being the crucial denominator:

> Black women, at least the Black women I have come in contact with in the movement have been expounding all their energies in 'liberating' Black men (if you yourself are not free, how can you 'liberate some one else?) Consequently, the movement has practically come to a standstill…We have found that Women's Liberation is an extremely emotional issue, as well as an explosive one. Black men are still parroting the master's prattle about male superiority…It is really disgusting to hear Black women talk about giving Black men their manhood—or allowing them to get it. This is degrading to other Black women and thoroughly insulting to Black men (or at least it should be). How can someone 'give' one something as

> personal as one's adulthood? That's precisely like asking the beast for your freedom. We also chew the fat about standing behind our men. This forces me to question: Are we women or leaning posts and props? It sounds as if we are saying if we come out from behind him, he'll fall down. To me, these are clearly maternal statements and should be closely examined.[9]

Thus, Men's Lib, with its emphasis on freeing men from the illusions of superiority and fixed notions about gender roles, seems to be as valid and compulsory necessity among the marginalised communities as it might be for those holding on to the centre of the things. The crucial question that it raises is that the individual man and woman have to take more responsibility in raising children, and more particularly their sons, which a socio-political movement may not be ready to accede to them as well recognise because of its own immediate necessities to assert community identities. May be some beginning, some balancing can be thought about because ultimately all socio-political assertions should end up giving power to decide and take decisions to individuals.

This is a revised, updated, and much expanded version of the article "Liberating' the Men" published in Media Spectrum, January 2008, under its 'Opinion' column.

CHAPTER 2

TAJ MAHAL AND THE IMAGE OF WOMANHOOD AND LOVE

Politics of Representation?

This essay underlines that the philosophical or the 'ideological' side of Taj Mahal—the fact it has stood for more than 350 years as a tribute to love and womanhood—has not been 'touched'. It seeks to highlight that in the backdrop of Post-colonial and Feminist discourses which have now been able to underline how down the ages, 'image-making' and the 'politics of representation' have been one of the major tools to establish the superiority of the dominant over subaltern, male over female, the great Taj can very well be seen as a tool of the perpetuation of male notions about what the right womanhood or love should be.

'Branding' of Mumtaz Mahal as an 'Ideal' Wife

It may be jarring to suggest, but a close scrutiny of the historical facts and our social attitudes does bear out that since at the centre of this monumental gift lies a loving, doting, and traditional wife like Mumtaz Mahal *nee* Arjumund Banu, it might have come handy to reinforce traditional male/society's conception of womanhood. The question that arises in one's mind is whether the Taj would have derived this much of attention and praise had it been made in the memory of an independent minded, freedom seeking and 'feminist' personalities like a Razia Sultana, or a Noor Jahan? Actually, the romantic, dreamy and tragic background of the construction of Taj Mahal have been so overpowering and so skilfully played up that one finds even the most feminist or liberated woman of our time to be quite oblivious of the way the image of Mumtaz Mahal as an ideal woman has been able to score over some of the strong female personalities as mentioned above without any discussion on the status of Mumtaz Mahal as an individual.

It is hardly surprising then that while we talk about the death of Mumtaz Mahal in 1631 and the way it left Shahjahan emotionally derelict leading him to the construction of the mausoleum, we just gloss over the fact the she died while delivering his 14th child, a daughter called Dahar Ara, in the span of 19 years of marriage having got married in 1612. It is not surprising that seven of the children died in infancy.

Here one can very well refer to the eminent feminist critic Madhu Kishwar's analysis of the way 'the pervasive popular cultural ideal of womanhood' has been sustained through the image of a 'woman as a selfless giver, someone who gives and gives endlessly, gracefully, smilingly, whatever the demand, however unreasonable and harmful to herself'.[1] The image of Mumtaz Mahal is certainly a case in point sustained through the powerful symbol of Taj Mahal with the romantic angle woven around it.

Considering the royal customs of the time, it is not worth discussing that Mumtaz Mahal was not the only woman in Shahjahan's life—though it is commonly accepted that she was the 'favourite' queen. However, for the sake of record, the names[2] of his other queens like the Izz-un-Nisa Begum (also called Akbarabadi Mahal), who made large red stone mosque at Faizbazar in Delhi in 1651 and a masjid at Agra called Akbarabadi Masjid; Fatehpuri Begum, the founder of the Fatehpuri Masjid at Delhi; Qandahari Begum (buried at Qandahari Bagh in Agra); Kabuli Mahal; Sarhindi Begum etc may be taken.

Despite the all too common practice of polygamy mostly followed by the male of the royalty down the ages (however the concession to the female to re-marry in case of death of the husband or estrangement or out of sheer love can also be exemplified), one finds that an intelligent woman like Noor Jahan *nee* Mehr-un-Nisa, one of the wives of Jahangir, could command ultimate power and rise much beyond the status of a decorative woman in the life of the king.

It is of common knowledge that during the last years of Jahangir, it was her word that was law with the Emperor largely managing the affairs of the state in her 'consultation'. When we are confronted with the fact that she was the only woman during the Mughal period whose name accompanied that of the king on the *farmans* as well as coins of the day with the inscriptions like, *by order of the emperor Jahangir, gold acquired a hundred times additional value by the name of the empress Nur Jahan*[3], we can gauge for sure the paramount importance she held during the time.

However, the facts that Nur Jahan almost ruled the country with elan, that she was gifted with the rare quality of composing extempore verse, that she invented the device to perform attar distillation from flowers to make perfumes, and also came up with many innovations in food, jewellery and dress etc are not the ones which are etched in popular imagination. Her name generally evokes the image of a cruel, obstinate, and vindictive woman who quelled any rebellion against the dynasty forcefully. Interestingly, the general impression has been that since Jahangir mostly whiled away his time in hunting, womanising, wine-drinking etc, it provided Nur Jahan the right opportunity to become the *de facto* ruler. How about looking at her from the perspective of a woman who stepped in, took control and saved the dynasty from dissipating despite a pleasure-seeking king and husband?

The fact that Jahangir was her second husband has also seemed to have gone against her. The different yardsticks that have been employed to judge a man and woman for the same kinds of behaviour or misbehaviour are quite glaring in the case of Nur Jahan vis-à-vis other male rulers. It is surprising to note that in the context of a male ruler his cruelty, impulsive behaviour, brutal suppression of rebellion etc are seen and explained in terms of social and political phenomena, in the context of someone like Nur Jahan, that becomes personal characteristics, unbecoming of the female of the species. Is not it so because she fails to fit in the picture of a subordinate and docile wife as Mumtaz Mahal does? It becomes all the more ironic when we realise that Mumtaz Mahal was the daughter of Nur Jahan's brother Asaf Khan, the all important vizier of Shahjahan.

The 'virtues' of power, adultery, rebellion etc in the case of a man metamorphosises into a clear cut vice or as the most dominating feature in the case of a woman.[4] This seems to have been the motivating factor in creating a particular kind of image of Razia Sultana also, who actually became the Empress of India (1236–1240) under Slave Dynasty during Delhi Sultanate era almost three hundred years before the founding of the Mughal Empire in 1526. It is interesting to note that when historians have found it rather a difficult proposition to even list out the names of all the 'legal' wives of the kings and Sultans down the ages due to obvious reasons, even the 'details' of the so-called romantic liaison of Razia Sultana with one Abyssinian slave, Jalaluddin Yaqut, have survived all these more than 750 years after her demise!

Is not it an androcentric perspective on history which has given too much importance to this aspect of Sultana's life as seen in discussions among historians on issues such as whether Yakut used to lift Sultana in his arms to make her sit on horse and whether this infuriated the medieval lords around her? Consequently, any mention of the reign of Razia Sultana brings to the popular mind the sensual image of a Sultana flirting allegedly publicly with a black slave. This has of course been exploited and re-emphasised by the popular Hindi movie made on her. Needless to say that the fact that she was probably the first woman to ascend the throne of Delhi who worked a lot in promoting education in her brief and turbulent reign has been given a short shrift.

One reason for this kind of treatment to her may also be due to the fact that in the society dominated by men, she took the battle right into the very male bastions—dressing and behaving in a masculine way. Her decision to enter into marital alliance with the governor of Bhatinda, Malik Altunia, who had rebelled against her, to unsuccessfully save her throne, can very well be seen as the unequivocal assertion of her sexuality to achieve political ends, which had always been the male preserve.

Naturally, one can be very much sure that in our 'modern', for that matter 'post-modern' age, the enterprise of someone like Razia Sultana or Nur Jahan, who had the 'temerity' to rule over the feudal, male dominated society in their respective periods and respective ways; who could assert their self, is unlikely to be a role model even now. For the contemporary man, the husband-centric persona of Mumtaz Mahal is likely to be more desirable because on her he can shower the praises of beauty and love from his own secure pedestal of confirmed superiority over his 'beloved'. In the contemporary jargon, it can be seen as a preference for an 'educated, decent housewife' by an Indian male over 'career minded, ambitious working woman.'

In this context, one cannot but bring to evoke the proverb from Mozambique that says 'never marry a woman with big feet'[5] which is likely to be accepted by most of the 'modern' men.

Woman as 'Beloved'

This brings us to the politics of love as a domain of man, where invariably woman is the 'beloved' and not vice-versa. And even in instances, where the man is the 'beloved', the woman's existence and freedom depends on the man she desired. This issue has been quite admirably studied and discussed by Neela Bhattacharya Saxena.[6]

However, in the context of discussing Taj Mahal as a symbol of love, it is neither desirable nor proper to draw parallels from literature, mainly because the contemporary history itself can provide suitable illustration. The question raised in the second paragraph of this write-up can very well have a corollary: Would Taj Mahal have become a symbol of love had a woman made it for her 'beloved'? The question becomes quite relevant in the context of the historical background to the making of another splendid and more pioneering mausoleum of the Mughal period, Humayun's Tomb at Delhi.

Made during Akbar's reign, its construction was started in 1565 and it took almost 16 years in its completion. The surprising and the sad part of this beautiful building is the fact that it was actually built under the initiative and supervision of Humayun's widow Hamida Bano Begum or Haji Begum (who was Humayun's companion in his Persian exile[7] and mother of Akbar) has not found favour in the popular folklore unlike the 'love story' associated with the Taj. In fact, it has now become customary to refer to Humayun's Tomb as having been built by the Emperor Akbar perhaps because it appears to be more 'appropriate' than blowing up the angle of a woman making it in the memory of her husband. Catherine B. Asher points out this appropriation well when she remarks,

> Tradition states that a devoted wife Hajji Begum was responsible for its (Humayun's Tomb's) construction, recently however Akbar has been proposed as the patron (Glenn Lowry) even though the tomb resembles none of Akbar's other architectural enterprises.[8]

It becomes all the more glaring when we find that the critics of architecture like Asher, Papadopoulo, Douglas Mannering etc pointing out that the paradisiacal imagery of Taj Mahal, as also the basic architecture of the central hall with its dome surrounded by four small cupolas etc, all primarily take after Humayun's Tomb. In that sense Taj Mahal has not been found to be an 'experimental' architecture as Mannering states, "Its (Taj Mahal's) plan was not new but based on the tomb of ShahJahan's great grandfather Humayun."[9] However, what sets the Taj apart as an architectural marvel is the much bigger scale on which it was envisaged and constructed coupled with the fact that the splendid use of the white marble makes it utterly unbelievable.

How does one take that the 'love angle' to Humayun's Tomb has remained largely unnoticed? The comparison between Haji Begam and Shahjahan in the context of their expression of love for their respective spouses and the way Shahjahan's emotions have been blown up down the ages whereas those of Haji Begam's have been consigned to the footnotes of history, is the best example of what Virginia Woolf[10] in her essay *A Room of One's Own* (1929) describes as the sharp distinction between 'male' self-realization and 'female' self-annihilation that the human society has been based on. Considering the fact that the polygamous angle in the case of Haji Begum's (as like all kings Humayun also had many other wives) relationship with her husband was an imposed condition, while in the case of Shahjahan it was an adopted one, one can not have much of hesitation in stating that Haji Begam's desire to have a grand mausoleum erected in her husband's memory was purely an act of love.

This is a revised version of a paper that first appeared in AUGUST 2005 issue of the fortnightly MEDIA SPECTRUM published by Spectrum Books, New Delhi.

CHAPTER 3

INDIA: NATION-STATE VERSUS CIVILIZATION

Some Notes

In Shakespeare's *Hamlet*, the basic dilemma of the protagonist is how to act morally in an immoral world, as any action in the immoral world would necessarily involve oneself in immorality itself. For the contemporary post-colonial critics, whether in the field of literature or history or films or popular culture, the buzzword(s) is (are) the assessment of 'politics of knowledge' and 'image making' as perpetrated on the historically or culturally marginalized by the dominant down the ages that needs to be examined and re-examined from the perspective of the marginalized. However, for them, the dilemma should be how to examine the historical process of the 'politics of knowledge' without becoming its prey, because, like the typical Hamletian predicament, any dabbling with this politics must involve them in it.

The dilemma is actually not new for the community of intellectuals. All new creations take birth out of dissatisfaction with the existing works on a particular theme. Yet for the present highly polarized and highly politicized intellectual world, where all men of letters are men of action too, we need to remind ourselves of this even more pointedly. This reminder is the urgent need of the hour because there is a growing trend among the post-colonial culture studies critics to escape this dilemma and to turn the discourse into 'us' versus 'them' syndrome depending upon whatever poles of social, political, cultural, gender or class one might be holding on to.

These prefatory remarks are crucial in the context of the review of the present book because while it starts out with asking right questions on the status and motive of contemporary culture studies, it falters immediately thereafter when it seeks to come up with responses to these questions in the form of the essays that follow. There is no doubt that the Marxist scholars have dominated Indian intellectual scene since independence. As a result, a good part of the contemporary post-colonial culture evaluation in the country has two-pronged targets. While on the one hand, it tries to examine the lopsided colonial view about Indian culture and society; it also simultaneously directs its ire against the Marxist interpretation of the colonial view of such matters.

In so far as the questioning of the Marxist interpretations about Indian culture and society comes out of the inner restlessness to counter it in terms of the perceived 'wrong' analysis of the plural consciousness of the country, it is always welcome. However, if the counter analysis takes sustenance from certain prejudices that are ingrained in the Indian society, then it becomes quite problematic. Take, for example, the following passage from the Introduction to the book by the author Vinay Lal:

> Subaltern history has doubtless made many advances upon previous work in Indian history, but its incapacity to deal with religion is all too evident. A certain awkwardness with respect to religion afflicts much of the secular Indian intelligentsia, and it is notable that those who purport to be religious-minded, such as the adherents of Hindutva ideology, are just as uncomfortable with Hinduism. The Hindutvavadis derive their teachings from Veer Savarkar, who was eminently secular: he had only disdain for that fuzzy, unbounded, multi-pronged, and largely unregulated religion called Hinduism. The secularists, it is true, have no interest in creating the conditions that would lead to a Hindu nation-state, but nonetheless they share with their putative opposites a similar indifference to matters of faith. Cultural studies, in whatever shape or form is spectacularly devoid of religious or even spiritual and – as shall become clear—civilizational moorings.

There are certain basic flaws in this line of argument. First, the debate is raked up on the lines of secular vs. religious, which actually presents secularism as something opposed to religion. In Indian society, and in the contemporary India, more so, secularism is propagated as a kind of liberal response to the issue of religion in personal as well as public life. A secular person can be non-religious or even areligious, but not anti-religious. In the same way as a religious person can be non-secular or asecular but not anti-secular. To be secular is to deal with the issue of religion in terms of religion, and not something away from it or something against it. A religious and a secular both actually draw their sustenance from the same spiritual source of co-existence and tolerance. Gandhi was the man who showed through personal example how the secular and religious derive sustenance from the common source of mutual respect.

Also, the author tries to further the general politically expedient conviction of the feasibility of the dichotomy of the public and private postures pertaining to one being secular. Can one be communal, a rabble-rouser in the name of religion and still be secular or for that matter religious in personal life? It is a question that stirred a hornet's nest some years back (and keeps coming back to us) regarding the so-called secular credentials of Jinnah and stares in our face on a daily basis.

Naturally, the author is not interested in any such debate, for despite the claims of the book containing essays on contemporary India, it is actually India's past that fascinates him more than its present. He states:

> As a civilization, India has an enviable history—part of that history, stretching back to some 4000 years, and perhaps more, was to remain indifferent to historical productions and to the historical sensibility… As a nation-state, India is slightly more than 50 years, and its bark is much worse than its bite.

In the context of post-colonial and contemporary culture studies, such a statement is actually anti-climax of sorts. In fact, this tendency to belittle the achievements of the modern, democratic, progressive, secular and cosmopolitan India as it has endeavoured to emerge since its independence (not only 'in spite of' but also 'because of' its civilizational moorings) unconsciously puts the author among the company of the Orientalists of the colonial period who harked back upon India's past while remaining indifferent to its immediate present and its concerns thereof.

Some clues to this indifference to India's present and some kind of romantic and almost vague fascination for the India of yore can be found in the kind of audience that these essays are seeking. All these essays written between 1995–2000 appeared in various journals abroad, mainly American. This is understandable as the author teaches history at the University of California, Los Angeles. However, this also means that author is more interested in addressing an audience outside India. Naturally, this lends a special colour, rather a special tension to the overall tone of the essays.

And tension is reflected in the way the author takes up issues that would not attempt to go much beneath the core debates plaguing the contemporary India and continue to occupy the most important socio-political and intellectual space in the country since the crucial transitional phase of 1989–1991 even though all these essays were written in its aftermath: the issues of militant Hindutva, dynamics of dalit assertion and quite importantly, the issues of economic reforms & globalisation. There actually appears to be some kind of contempt for the very idea of India as a nation-state, which, according to the author, feeds upon things like obsession with Guinness Book of Records, concerns about the security of Indian VIPs and equating of games like cricket with 'wars'.

Though these are certainly the part of contemporary Indian reality, but is that the whole truth of the progress of India as a nation-state? It is rather strange that the author would like to hark back upon the intrinsic qualities of India as a civilization while remaining completely oblivious of the suppression and discrimination that kept that idea going which has precisely been the focus of attention of India as a nation-state. In essay after essay, these notions keep coming up like a lament of a soul completely oblivious to or deliberately indifferent to the dynamics and inevitability of the positive alterations being brought about by India as a nation-state to India as a civilization.

One example of the way author views civilization vs. nation-state issue can bear out that as a historian he is actually trying to be an Orientalist, though, perhaps, at the terms of the Oriental, and perhaps that is what saves these engaging essays from sliding into the morass of through and through Western view of India. In this sense, the essays belong to the genre of, what may be termed as,

Neo-Orientalism, where all socio-political issues are to be treated under the ambience of culture and civilization albeit removed from the kinetic changes it must embrace. In the last essay on 'The Bittersweet Sweets of Modernity: Cricket and the South Asian Sensibility', wherein the author sees the intense battle of Indian and Pakistani cricket teams on field supported equally intensely by respective countrymen as a manifestation of the depravity brought about by the system of nation-state, he states:

> Though the nation-state...is firmly tethered to discourses of history and science as it came to be shaped in the modern West, a civilization entertains a notion of the plurality of sciences, just as it is more hospitable to non-historicist and ahistoricist modes of comprehension and narration, whether construed as folktales, prophecy, oral literatures, proverbs, mythological tales, epics, puranas, or mother's wit.

In this sense, the author endeavours to make his own path of the analysis of contemporary Indian issues which are best manifested in two essays titled 'Gandhi and the Ecological Vision of Life: Too Deep for Deep Ecology and 'Not This, Not That: The Hijras of India and the Cultural Politics of Sexuality'. However, one would hope that this path would also gradually mature into acceding much more dignified status to the evolution of India as a nation-state, which despite the alterations it must bring to the idea of India as a civilization, has actually been deeply guided by that very plural idea, a point that the author seeks to de-emphasise.

This is a slightly modified version of BOOK REVIEW of the title 'Of Cricket, Guinness and Gandhi: Essays on Indian History and Culture' by Vinay Lal (Penguin Books India in association with Seagull Books, 2005, 228pp, Rs. 295 (PB), ISBN 0-14-400005-9) published in 'Indian Literature', November-December 2005 issue (no. 230), by Sahitya Akademi.

CHAPTER 4

NATIONAL CONSCIOUSNESS AND THE 'BIHAR MOVEMENT'

A Reading of Babu Brajakishore Prasad's Presidential Address at Bihar Students' Conference, Chapra, 1911

The presidential address of Babu Brajkishore Prasad* at the 1911 session of the sixth Bihar Students' Conference—which took place annually during Dasahara[1] period—needs to be seen in its transitional, historical context. First of all, the speech takes place in 1911, when one of the most important missions of Babu Brajkishore Prasad's public life and that of his other eminent contemporaries from Bihar, was about to become a reality.

---

* Brajkishore Prasad (1877–1946) was a lawyer and an eminent leader of the Indian National Movement, and a close associate of Mahatma Gandhi, who devoted a full chapter in his *Autobiography* on Prasad under the heading 'The Gentle Bihari'. The text of Prasad's 1911 Address was made available through Bihar Archives, Patna.

The mission, of course, was the carving out of Bihar from Bengal and making it a separate province. The issue of Bihar was settled with the Delhi Durbar proclamation in December 1911, cancelling the Partition of Bengal as announced in 1905. The separation of Bihar from Bengal was a great historical feat as it freed the Hindi-speaking areas of Bengal from one layer of colonial and cultural subjugation and allowed for them a socio-political identity and space in the newly emerging national consciousness under the one geographical, economic, social and cultural entity called Bihar, then written as Behar.

However, the movement for the creation of Bihar, was not an easy task for its leaders. In fact, those espousing the cause of Bihar were seen to be moving in the opposite direction of the clarion call for national unity that was gradually enveloping the Indians, in general, and educated Indians, in particular. No wonder, Sachchidanand Sinha (1871–1950), in his article on Mahesh Narayan (1858–1907), another pioneering leader of the Bihar Movement, rather painfully recorded how the leaders of the Bihar movement were considered almost 'anti-national' by the intelligentsia of Bengal as well as of other parts of the country for espousing their cause. It may be instructive to quote him to make out the moral dilemma that was posed before them and how they successfully held their ground:

> Readers of Bryce's *American Commonwealth* are no doubt aware that there exists in the United States a strong state patriotism, which subsists side by side with federal patriotism. This was precisely our ideal, but it was unfortunately not at all appreciated in Bengal—then the predominant partner in the Lower Provinces—as its practical effect was the setting up of now well-known cry for 'Bihar for Biharees'. In some other provinces, too, this ideal was regarded by some as 'anti-national', but such a view was not at all well-founded. As a matter

> of fact, the intense excitement, some years later on Bengal having sundered by the Curzonian partition (under which scheme two-thirds of the Bengalees shared, as its result, a common administration with the Assamese, and the remaining one-third with the Biharees and the Oriyas) conclusively established that our ideal of linguistic provinces in India based on a common language, and also on historic traditions and territorial patriotism, was absolutely right. [2]

One can very well understand the pain and dilemma which Sinha underlines above because the perception that Bihar movement did not have support at the national level has percolated down to contemporary history writings too and much of it can be attributed to the lack of research about the Movement at the micro level. One can refer to the following observation to illustrate this:

> The birth of politics in Bihar, in the proper sense of the term, is connected with a cause, which, *although it was not popular,* was sponsored by the intellectuals. This was the issue of separation of Bihar from Bengal.[3] (italics added)

It is, thus, no coincidence that in the present address, Babu Brajkishore Prasad first of all takes up the issue of the rationale of having such a students' conference. This is certainly the direct result of the questioning which he and other leaders of Bihar had had to undergo as indicated above. At the same time, however, his address seems to be infused with a sense of optimism for the future of his province, mainly because of the imminent separation of Bihar from Bengal. The main starting para of the address, following the introductory one in which he comes out as a very humble personality before the students, needs to be quoted in full to appreciate these conflicting emotions that seemed to have guided his address:

> Gentlemen, the necessity and advisability of holding a students' conference has been questioned in some quarters. It is doubted by some

> whether a conference of students like yours is of any real utility. It is easy to doubt and criticize work. I would like to tell those gentlemen, who seem to know very little of the aims and object, as also of the workings, of your Conference, that of all the public associations or conferences in our province, or in any other province of this country, if there is one which, more than others, serves a really useful purpose, it is your Conference. It has given a new life to the students of Behar. It has infused a new spirit in them. The overflowing enthusiasm, the robust optimism, the mutual sympathy and fellow-feeling, the organized co-operation, and above all, the spirit de-corps which I see in you today in all the works of the Conference. You, gentlemen, who are the further hopes of the country, are receiving very good and valuable training through your Conference; and when you have left off your student-life and entered the world, you will find yourselves more fitted, more equipped, more ready and more willing to fight the battle of the country than the present generation which is engaged in it did actually find itself at the same stage. You will make better citizens of the British Empire and be better capable of doing good to your country and to yourself than we have been. By the time you finish your student career you will have learnt much which those who have gone before you had to learn for many a year after they had entered life. What can be a better justification than all for the existence of your Conference? Let those who doubt open their eyes, and examine the thing more closely and they will be satisfied that yours is a very useful institution.

The exhortation of Babu Brajkishore Prasad to the students of the Conference to 'become better citizens of the British Empire' is in line with the general belief among the contemporary intelligentsia about the British rule being the harbinger of modern and progressive education and ideas, and it is not at all odd that he uses expressions like:

> Thanks to the British Government which has kept us alive! All praise to the English people who have educated us! All honour

> to the British statesmen who have given us peace and made the realization of our future hopes possible!

In fact, if we compare these expressions to the ones used by Bishan Narayan Dhar during his Presidential Address of the Indian National Congress at Calcutta in 1911 itself, we would be able to better understand the mood and expectations of the intelligentsia from the British educational system at the time:

> English education and a closer contact with the West have raised our intelligence and expanded our vision; the example of English enterprise has given us new ideals of citizenship and inspired us with new conception of national culture.[4]

'De-political' Message of the Address

Another factor that needs to be underlined is the rather complete absence of political message to the students in terms of any anti-colonial content. Babu Brajkishore Prasad in the address focuses entirely on the educational and intellectual training of the youth of Bihar and the nation. And, in fact, the tone of the address shows him to be almost cautioning the students to not become avowedly political and remain focused as his following words show:

> Gentlemen, but yours is purely a student's conference, and I hope you will always keep it in mind and handle those matters only which concern you as students.

Rather, towards the end of the address, he touches upon the issue of students and politics directly as the 'last matter' and quite obliquely conveys how getting 'sound education' in itself should be seen as the most important political 'dharma', so to say:

> The last matter to which I wish to draw your attention is the question of students and politics. I have given my most careful consideration to this matter and am in a position to tell you that I quite agree with those who ask you not to mix yourself up in the active politics of the day. It is very harmful to students. But this does not mean that you should shut your eyes to what is going on around you. Rather I would like to see you get a sound education in the principles of politics so that you may be able to play your part and play it well when the time arrives.

However, in order to understand this rather de-political line of argument adopted by an eminent politician before a conference of young students trying to acquire a new political identity in the form of Bihar and Biharee, we need to go to the genesis of the Bihar Students' Conference which was established in 1906 with Dr. Rajendra Prasad as one of the prime movers. And what better and authentic would be than to quote Dr. Rajendra Prasad himself who touches upon this issue in his *Autobiography:*

> While the rules and regulations were being drafted, I remember that two points were hotly discussed: (1) whether the Conference should take part in politics and (2) whether the conference should be confined to Behari students only or thrown open to Bengali students also.
>
> There was a difference of opinion on the first point and the elders opposed participation in politics. Wisely, as it seems now, the Conference decided that it would not take part in political agitation. At that time, Bihar was part of Bengal. Educationally it was backward, and had hardly any public life. Only a small section of the people was supporting the Congress. Bihar had no political organization of its own and the Congress had not yet set up its branches there. The Students' Conference, though dominated by youth, was the first platform where Biharis met to discuss questions of common

> interest. In these circumstances, if we had not proceeded cautiously, the Conference perhaps would not have been the success it was.[5]

The 'elders' mentioned by Rajendra Prasad could very well have been leaders like Brajkishore Prasad, Sachchidanand Sinha, Mahesh Narayan etc, whose insistence to have a de-political orientation for the Bihar Students' Conference was certainly a political decision in itself. What the Bihar students' Conference achieved was the sustained and not-so-pronounced political training in the initial years for the students of the newly emerging socio-political aspirations of Bihar. Babu Brajkishore Prasad's exhortation to the students to 'get a sound education in the principles of politics so that you may be able to play your part and play it well when the time arrives', proved to be prophetic as during the Champaran movement, as pointed out by Rajendra Prasad in his *Autobiography*, the volunteers who worked with Gandhiji, Brajkishore Prasad, Rajkumar Shukla, Rajendra Prasad and other leaders were drawn from the ranks of the Students' Conference and they really played their part heroically when the time arrived for it. In fact, it may be worthwhile to mention that for the next nearly two decades, all major political and national movement leaders from Bihar were products of the Students' Conference only.

Pitching for Scientific As Well As Passionate Approach

The 1911 Presidential Address of Babu Brajkishore Prasad stands out for the wide range of issues that he takes up to sort of initiate the attending students into major contemporary discourses. First, he emphasizes on and impresses upon the students about the need to develop a scientific approach to appreciate phenomena like, say, the spread of education in Bihar, by basing their understanding and analysis on facts and figures. What he tries to drive home at seems to be valid even today because of the still-prevalent tendencies among public figures to make sweeping observations without relating them to scientifically collated data and statistics:

> I would like to impress upon you that the first and foremost question which your Conference should take up is the spread and growth of education in Bihar. Has there been a steady increase in education, or a decrease in it in the province? I have heard some people say that the number of Bihari graduates turned out these days is fewer than what used to be the case ten years before. Is this a fact? Is it true? Your Conference should ascertain it; and the best means your Conference can adopt is to take statistics of two decennial periods, i.e., from 1891 to 1900 and from 1901 to 1910, and see where we are. If you find the result unfavourable or not so favourable as it ought to be, you should try to find out the causes at the root and remedy them.

This point also stems from the analytical training that the leaders like Babu Brajkishore Prasad would have liked the young generation of Bihar to imbibe in order to take forward the cause of the socio-economic and political development of their people in a more methodical manner. It needs to be mentioned that during the last two decades, the leaders from Bihar—and Babu Brajkishore Prasad was in the forefront of such leadership—had to come up with painfully collected data and statistics to demand better facilities and infrastructure for the people of Bihar from the Bengal administrative apparatus in the areas of education, health, sanitation, poverty alleviation etc. Being a torchbearer of the cause of Bihar, Babu Brajkishore Prasad knew it too well the long and intricate road ahead for the progress of the people of Bihar, which had less than 5% of literacy in 1911, and how much of preparedness and training it demanded of the educated young men and women of Bihar.

Secondly, the point of spread of education and the huge resources that it required is taken up in the address. Though the rich 'Maharajas and Rajas, Nawabs and Noblemen' are exhorted to help in the cause of education, but by suggesting the creation of sort of a co-operative of Bihari Students' Fund to help the poor students pursue education, Babu Brajkishore Prasad is able to underline the need for the better off students to identify with the lot of the underprivileged as well and be actively empathetic to their needs. It is interesting to note that the eminent and successful lawyer as well as statesman that he was, Babu Brajkishore Prasad pitches for the twin approach of scientific as well as passionate engagement with the problems of the contemporary life as the ideal to be adopted by the upcoming educated generation of Bihar and the country.

Issues that Still Plague Us: Technical Education, Ignorance of the Past, Hindi-Urdu Chasm, Development of Indian Languages through Translations

In the later part of his address, Babu Brajakishore Prasad touches upon three major issues afflicting the educational, social as well as cultural fabric of Bihar, which, unfortunately are yet to be settled satisfactorily and have rather acquired a more complex character. The first important concern that is taken up is the one relating to the deplorable status of technical education in Bihar. In fact, more than the lack of technical institutions in Bihar, Babu Brajakishore Prasad hits at the lack of interest as well as awareness among the students of Bihar about benefits of technical education for a society. As he puts it:

> The Government naturally solicitous of our welfare established two technical institutions at Patna, viz. the Bihar School of Engineering and the Patna Temple Medical School. But it is a pity that we have

> not been yet able to take full advantage of these institutions. The fault is ours. Even to day the majority of students in the Bihar School of Engineering are non-Biharees.

Though the concerns of Babu Brajakishore Prasad about the appalling situation of technical education, especially in the context of Bihar and its students, were worthwhile, but it appears that this was one issue that plagued other parts of India too in varying degree, but with equal intensity. It may be instructive to refer to A.R. Desai who refers to the scenario prevalent as later as 1934–35:

> The economic development of a backward country demands educational cadres trained in technical studies. In 1934–35, the students graduating in engineering, agriculture or commerce numbered only 960.[6]

Immediately thereafter, Desai goes on to quote from D. H. Buchanan's seminal study *The Development of Capitalist Enterprise in India* (1934) thus:

> The greatest shortage has been in technical education. In such fields as agriculture, commerce and engineering, one sparsely settled American state such as Iowa, with one per cent of the population of British India, has more students.[7]

Having said this, one can't but marvel at the visionary social diagnosis offered by Babu Brajkishore Prasad in the very initial stages of the making of Bihar as well as that of national awakening by emphasizing on the importance of technical education for bringing about national self-reliance. His message to the students attending the conference thus has historical significance for flagging emergent educational concerns as one of the basic objectives before the Bihar Students' Conference in order to do 'immense good to the country':

> I think it the duty of your Conference to create in the Bihar student an interest in technical education and to popularize it by all means among them. This you can do by pointing out to them the advantage of this sort of education and by supplying to them all the necessary information as regards the technical institutions situated in different parts of the country. If you succeed in doing this, you will have done immense good to the country.

Another issue that engages his mind and is something which the Indian society is yet to reconcile with completely is the issue of lack of knowledge or perception about its own past or history and rather baffled approach to its culture. When Babu Brajakishore Prasad utters the following words, it becomes difficult to analyse them at face value because they carry with them various complex and subtle layers in which Indian history has unfolded before us, and in many ways, presented itself before the generation of Babu Brajakishore Prasad too nearly a century ago:

> Our education should be on national lines. Unless you know your past history, unless you study the ancient civilization of your country, unless you have in you the pride of your race, you will never be a true Indian. It is a pity, gentlemen, that most of our university graduates who can discuss for hours together the history of Europe are absolutely ignorant of the most important events in the history of their own country. They can very well delineate to you the causes that led to the American War of Independence or the French Revolution, but would look quite blank if asked about the causes or the effects on the country of the great-war on the fields of Kurukshetra. They can talk glibly about Fredrick the Great or Peter of Russia, but do not know the names of those who built up the great empire of the Saracens. They would be able to trace very accurately the genealogy of our late Queen Empress Victoria the Good from William the Conqueror, but

would miserably fail if asked to say who the Pandavas and the Kauravas were. They would enumerate very quickly the French or English authors of the last century, but would not be able to name even one Hindi or Urdu author of the same period. This is, gentlemen, true denationalization.

The seeds of 'denationalization' and cultural dichotomy of the educated Indians that the above quoted passage show were practically laid down in the first half of the 19th century itself, when the British, then ruling through the East India Company, gradually started making some policies in the fields of culture and education and could bring themselves to set aside some limited budget for the same. Prof. Bipan Chandra puts this all very succinctly and in its proper historical context:

> For years a great controversy raged in the country on the question of the direction that this expenditure should take. While one section of opinion wanted it to be spent exclusively for the promotion of modern Western studies, others desired that, while western sciences and literature should be taught to prepare students to take up jobs, emphasis should be placed on the expansion of traditional Indian learning. Even among those who wanted to spread Western learning differences arose on the question of medium of instruction to be adopted in modern schools and colleges. Some recommended the use of Indian languages, called vernaculars at the time, for the purpose, while others advocated the use of English. Unfortunately, there was a great deal of confusion on this question. Many people failed to distinguish between English as a medium and English as a subject of study and between Indian languages as a medium and traditional Indian learning as the main object of study.
>
> The two controversies were settled in 1835 when the Government of India decided to devote limited resources it was willing to spare to

> the teaching of Western sciences and literature through the medium of English language alone.[8]

The generation of Babu Brajkishore Prasad also grappled with this dichotomous nature of the spread of English education which they saw as the harbinger of hope as well as the one which was colonizing their mind as well as culture. The dichotomy, one can say, still prevails in the Indian society, and rather has been made part and parcel of the national progress and identity. In the present address of Babu Brajkishore Prasad, the talk of winning 'back the past glories of our ancient race', of regaining 'the honour of our country and people, and we shall once more be the guide of the whole human race' is immediately followed by praise for the British empire and their education system. However, therein he does not really betray any individual folly but only stands as a testimony to the making of a new kind of national consciousness which would strive to carry with itself both the traditional as well as the newly acquired modern ideas, which the enlightened men like Babu Brajkishore Prasad did carry through a harmonious amalgamation of the positive aspects of Indian traditions and those of the modern, western ideas of liberal socio-political outlook.

This amalgamation of the modern and the traditional is manifested in the concern for 'development of Hindi or you may call it Urdu'. In fact, when he states,

> for to me there does not seem to be any real difference between Hindi and Urdu. Of course I know that some people are trying to Sanskritise Hindi, while, others are equally trying to Persianise Urdu. Both of these are doing positive harm to the language itself and to the country.

Babu Brajkishore Prasad comes across as one of the most modern and mature statesmen of his times who could understand and express the need to have a plural approach to the emerging social realities in the North-India heartland, where the linguistic purity advocated by the both Hindi and Urdu fundamentalists contrary to the socio-historical processes were out to wreck a composite culture and polity at the turn of the 20th century. It is instructive to note that in the midst of the fierce battle that unfolded over the issue of the Sanskritisation of Hindi and Persianisation of Urdu, which ultimately took the communal turn of Hindu versus Muslim later greatly adding to the Partition of the country, Babu Brajkishore Prasad could find himself on the side of saner voices who tried to see the social, linguistic and grammatical affinities between Hindi and Urdu—one being poorer without the other and similarly one being enriched by the other when accepted as 'Hindustani', though he prefers to call the amalgamated language as 'Hindi'. His stress on translating texts and content into vernacular languages places him with the continued emphasis of the educated classes to enrich Indian languages through translations:

> I would impress upon those of you who have time and leisure to translate useful books in your own vernaculars, for this is the first step towards enriching any literature. The rise of a nation is measured by the development of its language and literature. To rise you should raise your language. Your conference can do much in this matter.

CHAPTER 5

'A FINISHED PRODUCT' OF INDIAN CULTURE CAUGHT IN THE CROSSFIRE OF COMMUNALISM

Maulana Azad as a 'Modern Dara Shikoh'

'Hero-Worship' is something that has time and again been derided by the intellectuals of all hues, and rightly so. But 'hero-worship' is also a phase of one's life. I have no hesitation in accepting that there are some personalities, for example, the poet-novelists, D H Lawrence and Nagarjun; the post-colonial critic Edward W. Said, about whom I am in the process of developing an intellectual detachment. I am sure, by and by, some kind of broader understanding would be developed to enable me to have that kind of detachment, as without 'doubt', one's faith in itself remains a doubtful thing. In this category of 'heroes', I will surely include Maulana Abul Kalam Azad (1888–1958), the first Education Minister of the independent India, but more importantly, one of the few stalwarts of national movement who could imbibe and contribute to the very essence of that elusive 'inclusive nationalism' that we nowadays are trying hard to figure out. I am no historian, but have deep interest in the historical process through which Indian civilization, in particular, has progressed, and hence the placement of Maulana Azad in Indian history, is very significant and runs deep into the secular and inclusive fabric.

However, C Rajagopalachari's description of Maulana Azad as 'The Great Akbar' of Modern India, quoted by the eminent historian Prof. Mushirul Hasan in an article in *The Hindu*[1] would akin to romanticizing Maulana's plight, and overlooking his tragedy. In fact, if at all he needs to be compared with any other figure from the Medieval period, it can be no other than Dara Shikoh. Because, while, the 'Emperor' Akbar was successful in establishing an empire that he wished to as per his multi-cultural vision of the country, Maulana Azad was almost 'sidelined' like Dara Shikoh, because he found himself at the crossfire of the majority and minority brands of communalism, where, like Mahatma Gandhi, his voice of sanity had few takers when it really mattered. Actually, Dara Shikoh is a tragic symbol of Hindi-Muslim unity, and Maulana Azad's position makes him nearer to that of Sanskrit-Persian poet-scholar, and brother of Aurangzeb, because, despite his life-long struggle, he, as other champions of Hindu-Muslim unity, could not avert the Partition of the country and the mass-tragedy that followed it.

To take this discussion further, when I say, 'few takers', I mean those whose voice counted, because the silent majority was very much with Maulana Azad. This has been so very suitably demonstrated by the historian Prof. Rizwan Qaiser in his book[2] *Resisting Colonialism and Communal Politics: Maulana Azad and the*

Making of the Indian Nation, and also articulated in this interview in *The Times of India*[3] wherein he stated:

> The Muslim League used to describe Azad and people belonging to the Azad Muslim Conference as "half-hearted pseudo-nationalists". What's important is that a vast majority of Muslims were not with the Muslim League in 1940–41. That's the most interesting part of my book...¦at the end of April 1940, about one lakh Muslims gathered in Delhi to say they're not a distinct nation and the Muslim League does not represent their interests. When Jinnah called Azad a 'show boy' of the Congress, it was rebuffed by many Muslims in Delhi and other places.

Jawaharlal Nehru referred to Maulana Azad, as the caravan leader, "a very brave and gallant gentleman, a finished product of the culture that, in these days, pertains to few". It certainly is an apt description of this great man, and we would do well to read again his historic Presidential speech made in 1940 at the Ramgarh Session of the Congress, wherein he provides a 'text' for understanding what nationalism and multi-culturalism should mean for us, and how it is intrinsically associated with both the rights *and* the duties of *both* the minorities and the majority—a very basic that seems to be under tremendous stress once again in our times. Moreover, the rather sophisticated approach to the question of religion, coming from a man who was a scholar of Islam, shows his visionary and intellectual integrity, on the one hand, and his abiding commitment to nationalism, on the other hand, in the most unambiguous manner:

> Full eleven centuries have passed by since then. Islam has now as great a claim on the soil of India as Hinduism. If Hinduism has been the religion of the people here for several thousands of years Islam also has been their religion for a thousand years. Just as a Hindu can

> say with pride that he is an Indian and follows Hinduism, so also we can say with equal pride that we are Indians and follow Islam. I shall enlarge this orbit still further. The Indian Christian is equally entitled to say with pride that he is an Indian and is following a religion of India, namely Christianity.[4]

What is remarkable, and that is why I perhaps find some kind of link among as varied people as D H Lawrence, Nagarjun, Edward Said and Maulana Azad, is their ability to recognize and put forth ambiguously that life is a two-way window, rather multi-way, and only the ones who can appreciate the same, can ever hope to contribute vibrantly, and alter meaningfully, the course of history, as each of them did in his chosen field of work.

CHAPTER 6

A GLOBAL CITY CALLED BOOK FAIR

An Insider's Attempt at Unraveling its Cartography

Many of us visit a book fair as a reader. But what about the perceptions of those whom we visit: the publishers, publishing professionals, trade and exhibition experts, stall designers–for them book fairs are like a one large global city with which they grow like insiders. Having had opportunities to participate as well as be part of organising teams for book fairs as well as holding of various literary programmes at different publishing destinations, this is my take on the phenomena of book fairs from that perspective.

The moment a publishing professional conversant with the maps of book fairs steps inside the hallowed precincts of a book fair, whether it is being held in an upward city Mall COEX in the heart of Seoul in the far-east or at the Earls Court of London on the other extreme of the globe or at Pragati Maidan in New Delhi or in the restless exhibition centre of Beijing or at the Frankfurt Trade Fair or at All-Russian Exhibition Centre, Moscow, he/she knows its lanes and by lanes like the palm of one's hand even though visiting it for the first time. Like some well-rehearsed exercise evoking *déjà vu*, one instantly finds one's way to the place of registration, looks for one's stalls in the directory for the sake of formality as one has already seen the layout and found out the placement of one's stall on the fair's website or has been already notified by the organisers, sets up books for display and gets ready for the rights meetings—fixed as well as walk-ins and impromptus—which many a time expect one to carry the unstated assignment of being cultural encyclopaedia of one's own country!

Large cut-outs of the book-covers of newly released titles, smiling bestselling and celebrity authors, octonorm stalls and stands of publishers and publishing associations, illustrators' walls, colourfully designed with innovative space utilisation booths of big publishers, buntings hanging overhead catching attention and a musical cacophony of visitors. Welcome to the Global City of Book Fairs–a city in itself with its own lanes and by lanes, structures, cultural and marketing space, codes and citizenship where language of books and people do not prove to be any barrier. In fact, the more the cultural and linguistic representations, the richer the City becomes, because citizens here speak the universal language of content creation, visual representation of ideas, and business of knowledge dissemination and are here to build bridges through the maze of multi-lingual, multi-cultural, multi-ethnic human discourses. No wonder, Brian Moeran, Professor of Business Anthropology in the Department of Intercultural Communication and Management at the Copenhagen Business School, Denmark, in his fine anthropological study on book fairs, states:

> With their sealed-in, windowless structure, their special stand constructions and furnishings, exhibition halls separate the book fair from the outside world. They also, as noted earlier, map out in spatial terms the key agents and institutions (different kinds of publishers, rights sellers, service providers, agents, media) within the field of publishing, and so embody that wider field as they produce, reproduce and legitimate both it and the positions of the players therein (cf. Entwistle and Rocamora 2006: 736).[1]

The best thing about this City is that it is not Utopian. It is grounded in deeper human reality of which the market reality is just a part. It can create avenues even for the smallest publishers publishing in languages spoken by a, say, handful, for example, Estonian, spoken by roughly 1 million people in this European nation of the Baltic region of the Northern Europe,and can have poets like Jaan Kapalinski and historical novelists like Jaan Kross whose works have been translated in all major languages across the world. Indeed, book promotion, the cherished ideals of this City, is all about promoting new ideas that carry human civilization on their shoulders.

The citizens of this City are, of course, novelists, poets, authors, translators, editors, linguists, grammarians, philosophers, illustrators, literary agents, rights managers, language interpreters, printers, academics, antiquarians, librarians, booksellers, journalists, software and multimedia suppliers and those selling plots in new settlement areas in the form of space at various international book fairs—all directly or indirectly serving the readers. But the best thing about the City of Book Fairs is that it gives faces to the names. Those connected via internet across the globe get to meet face-to-face in another fair.

These citizens see each other only in one book fair or the other and hence make themselves perfect inhabitants of it by emphasising that social and direct personal relations and networking are major function of the citizens of book fair. No wonder, its citizens attend the launch of the debut work of an author with the zest of birthday parties with the alliances between publishing houses working as contract marriages. As it happens, the resourceful and adventurous ones are able to find partners on their own, for some, matrimonial agencies specialising in 'match-making' have to make efforts to organise mass engagement possibilities through roundtables and talks!

Literary Festivals: A sub-city

Building upon these fabulous stories, interesting research have been undertaken to understand the sociological and economic rationale of the success of these direct, face-to-face alliances between publishers, between authors and readers, between authors and publishers and among them all.

At a Conference on *Book Cultures, Book Events: The Transnational Culture, Commerce and Social Impact of Literary Festivals* organised by University of Stirling, enlightening papers were read that could help one unravel the economics as well as the aesthetics of this City. Speaking on *Up Close and Personal: Why Readers love 'live' book events*, Danielle Fuller, Department of American & Canadian Studies, University of Birmingham, stated (in her abstract) in the context of UK, USA and Canada:

> The most successful mass reading events (MREs) – from Richard and Judy's Book Club to Canada Reads to long-running One Book, One Community programmes in Chicago and Kitchener-Waterloo-Cambridge – exploit the opportunities offered by the co-extensive relationships among media to produce multiple encounters with books. Equally significant to their success as entertainments, MREs

> extend the possibility for multiple encounters with other *people*. They provide opportunities for human interaction via a socially-networked event that can be engaged on- and off-line, either once or repeatedly. These encounters may be ephemeral, but, as our research has demonstrated, they are capable of producing significant moments of identification or affective connection among participants.[2]

In another enlightening paper on *The Future's Live, the Future's Digital: Why Publishers Should Embrace Live Events in a Digital Age* by Alastair Horne, Communities and Social Media Manager, Cambridge University Press, sought to underline the vital role that live interactive events with the authors at book fairs or at other literary festivals may play since the physicality of books is disappearing in some parts of the world where e-books have made a strong presence. I quote from her abstract:

> As ebook sales rise, economics may dictate that print itself will become a premium product: like vinyl, the preserve of enthusiasts for whom the physical object is a key part of the experience. I consider how the live event may add value here also, through such formats as exclusive souvenir editions packaged with the opportunity to meet the author.
>
> I explore how publishing might learn from the changing role that live events have played in the economics of the music industry. As the price of recorded music has dropped, live events are no longer a promotional tool for a recorded product but have become a premium product in their own right, and major artists now sign "360 deals" that package rights to tour and merchandising revenues alongside recording contracts – with both traditional record companies and new players. I examine how publishers might profitably follow suit.[3]

A Place for Cultural Makeovers

Yes, it is a democratic, liberal city run by the reading public for the reading public and by the reading public and its gates are getting opened up to new migrants. Let us find them out—film producers looking for scripts, regular special talks on transferring content from print to visual medium at Frankfurt show; organisations like Army looking for an image makeover as the stall of South Korean Army at Seoul International Book Fair or such pavilion at Livre Paris showed. When I asked the representative of South Korean Army stall in 2012 what they intended to achieve, its spokesperson said they wanted to show that joining army did not mean that you did not get to read and hence they had coined the slogan, 'make books your cruise missiles' and were accepting donations for their libraries.

In recent times, the international business centres like Abu Dhabi or Sharjah or Bangkok have hired professionals from abroad and pumped in money to organise book fairs with the objective to shake off perceptions about themselves and go for cultural makeovers. In this context, it is interesting to read what Edward Nawotka had to say in his article in *Publishing Perspectives:*

> Book fairs seem to have a civilizing effect on a city. Ironically, they are most successful in cities that seem on the surface the least likely to support them. In the United States the largest and most influential book fairs don't take place in New York or San Francisco, the two cities most closely associated with book publishing, but in Miami and Los Angeles, cities best known for vice and Hollywood. And then there's the National Book Festival, which takes place in Washington D.C., and was started by former First Lady Laura Bush, who took the inspiration from the Texas Book Festival, which she had launched a half-dozen years earlier in Austin. Politics and literature are not always the coziest of bedfellows.[4]

A new wave of citizens comprise of those specialising in creating 'book arts'. They previously occupied the enclave dedicated to book illustrators in this City, but have now branched out, brought in installation artists, sculptors, musicians etc. along and have created their own residential areas. You find them most conspicuously in the Fair dedicated to children's books and YAs, that is the Young Adults, held at the cosmopolitan Italian college city, Bologna in Northern Italy. They have been able to add new dimensions— their stalls presented as an artist's studio, books nailed and put in chains to show angst against the banned and censored books, fast food vans to display books on cookery etc.

It is a modern, cosmopolitan City, no doubt, but since its economy and culture revolves around ideas, published as well as yet-to-be published, it traces its origin to the *most ancient* human past. No wonder, the City has opened up large Special Economic and Cultural Zones/Thematic Towns for its citizens to assert, explore and enrich their identities. Hence we have Christian Book Fairs across the world, World Sanskrit Book Fair at Bengaluru, International Antiquarian Book Fair at California, International Women's Book Fair held in London, International Islamic Book Fair held in various cities in India as well as abroad etc. Mention of that fabulous concept of Art Book Fairs happening at various places such as New York and London would be in the fitness of the things where the book art enclave of Book Fair seems to bloom into its own and make a powerful statement on the collaboration of visual arts and printed books.

Those who think that this Global City is only about selling and buying (copy) rights, need to know that this City is founded on the premise of creating space for the other kinds of Rights too which make human civilization worth living and hoping for. Moreover, it also underlines that for all love stories to continue and sustain, physical proximity makes up for an essential part, whether with human beings or with books—a lesson that has been most tragically taught by the Covid Pandemic which impacted this city the most and from which its citizens are now struggling to get over slowy, but, perhaps, surely.

The original article was written for author's blog on the occasion of the opening of Frankfurt Book Fair, 2012.

CHAPTER 7

AN AMERICAN VIEW ON 'READING AS SOCIO-ECONOMIC SKILL'

Decoding Mr. Barack Obama's Views

While doing research for the first *National Youth Readership Survey*[1] some years back, among many new things that I stumbled upon, was one speech that Mr. Barack Obama, the then US Senator from Illinois (and later President of the United States of America), gave as a key-note address to the general session of the American Library Association's annual conference held in Chicago in June 2005. Relevant parts of the speech were quoted by the study team in the 'Looking Ahead' chapter of the report precisely because of the overpowering perspective it seemed to bring on the relationship between reading and socio-economic empowerment that it invariably gives to an individual. However, what struck me more was the sense of concern that an American politician could express at the lack of reading preparedness among its young people in the new millennium.

Mr. Obama's speech from his pre-Presidential days on reading as an individual's basic element to develop a wholesome understanding about oneself and one's surroundings is something that we can take as an important evidence, if at all any evidence was needed, of this time tested wisdom. The context of his speech is, no doubt, American, but considering that it takes generations for social behaviour indicators to show any perceptible change, we can take a few things out of the speech for its interpretation in the contemporary Indian context. Since the speech is made before the conference of librarians, hence the role of libraries is something that he keeps coming back to in the speech, but I am sure that the discerning reader will be able to make out that he is basically talking about reading as a basic tool for an individual to grow.

Hence when he utters the following lines, we know for sure that the critical reasoning and scientific temper that reading gives rise to among children is what he intends to drive home at while talking about the role of libraries in human societies:

> ...libraries remind us that truth isn't about who yells the loudest, but who has the right information. Because even as we're the most religious of people, America's innovative genius has always been preserved because we also have a deep faith in facts. And so the moment we persuade a child, any child, to cross that threshold into a library, we've changed their lives forever, and for the better. This is an enormous force for good.[2]

But what I like most is the historical and anthropological context in which he discusses the importance of reading, essentially for the American society, but which can be valid for any other society. Moreover, the speech goes beyond mere statements like 'books are our best friends' or 'books are mine of knowledge' etc that many make at such specialized gathering of professionals involved in book promotion without touching upon and underlining the tangible socio-economic advantages that it entails. To quote a bit in detail:

> …literacy is the most basic currency of the knowledge economy we're living in today. Only a few generations ago, it was okay to enter the workforce as a high school dropout who could only read at a third-grade level. Whether it was on a farm or in a factory, you could still hope to find a job that would allow you to pay the bills and raise your family.
>
> But that economy is long gone. As revolutions in technology and communication began breaking down barriers between countries and connecting people all over the world, new jobs and industries that require more skill and knowledge have come to dominate the economy. Whether it's software design or computer engineering or financial analysis, corporations can locate these jobs anywhere there's an internet connection. And so as countries like China and India continue to modernize their economies and educate their children longer and better, the competition American workers face will grow more intense; the necessary skills more demanding.
>
> These new jobs are about what you know and how fast you can learn what you don't know. They require innovative thinking, detailed comprehension, and superior communication…*Reading is the gateway skill that makes all other learning possible, from complex word problems and the meaning of our history to scientific discovery and technological proficiency. And by the way, it's what's required to make us true citizens.* In a knowledge economy where this kind of learning is necessary for survival, how can we send our kids out into the world if they're only reading at a fourth grade level? *(my emphasis)*

The interesting thing is the relationship that it draws between the reading needs of the young generation with their overall economic contribution. This is quite instructive for the socio-economic reality of a developing country like India too, where inculcation of reading habit is yet to seize the imagination of the society, mainly because book-hunger is something that can not become more overpowering than food-hunger in the Indian context. Secondly, in this light, it is further interesting to know how an American statesman looks at the societies like ours or China, believing them to be doing enough to 'modernize their economies and educate their children longer and better'.

It is no doubt, the part of India that seems to compete with the Americans is not the part that permeate the whole of India, but for an American politician that would not be of much relevance. Even during his Presidential years Mr. Obama talked highly about the arithmetic and language skills of children of Mumbai or those in Chinese metropolitan cities as compared to the children of USA. From the American perspective and from the issues related to the outsourcing of jobs, this makes sense for Mr. Obama to highlight. However, the basic statistics related to the reading-divide that exists between rich and poor, between black and white and so on and so forth that Mr. Obama quotes further down the speech should be able to connect with all those who are fighting for an inclusive learning society in India. It is indeed the data pertaining to the American society, if anybody who has ever been familiar with the realities of such a divide in India can find a homely echoe. To quote:

> Right now, one out of every five adults in the United States can't read a simple story to their child. During the last twenty years or so, over ten million Americans reached the 12th grade without having

> learned to read at a basic level. But these literacy problems start far before high school. In 2000, only 32% of all fourth graders tested as reading proficient. And the story gets worse when you take race and income into consideration. Children from low-income families score 27 points below the average reading level, while students from wealthy families score fifteen points above the average. And while only one in twelve white seventeen-year-olds has the ability to pick up the newspaper and understand the science section, for Hispanics the number jumps to one in fifty; for African Americans it's one in one hundred.

Moreover, when he highlights,

> It's not enough just to recognize the words on the page anymore - the kind of literacy necessary for 21st century employment requires detailed understanding and complex comprehension.

all those seeking to usher India into the 21st century as a superpower need to read this with lots of salt coming as it does from the leading political leader of the 'only' superpower—the dream model of many uninformed. At this stage, I need not quote numerous studies taking place in the education sector in India which underline the apparently insurmountable gaps that exists in terms of literacy, school-drop rates, non-availability of text books, etc to various sections of the society, because I am more interested in giving a critical view coming from the Mecca of the capitalist society just to understand if the road taken by them needs to be repeated whole hog as seem to be the whole time approach of some of the influential quarters.

Further, the one issue that seems to be impacting the whole culture of reading is the invasion of TV and internet in the society. To look at the view of Mr. Obama, brought up in a society that has been exposed to these technological invasions for generations, is to locate the need for course correction in our country which is just getting fully exposed to these technologies. To quote:

> When you're home, you might try to get your kids to read, but you're competing with the other byproducts of the technological revolution: video games and DVDs that they just have to have; TVs in every room of the household. Children eight to eighteen now spend three hours a day watching TV, while they only spend 43 minutes reading. Our kids aren't just seeing these temptations at home - they're everywhere. Whether it's their friends or the people they see on TV or a general culture that glorifies anti-intellectualism, *it's too easy for kids today to put down a book and turn their attention elsewhere. And it's too easy for the rest of us to make excuses for it - pretending that putting a baby in front of a DVD is educational, letting a twelve-year-old skip reading as long as he's playing good video games, or substituting dinner in front of the TV for family conversation. We know that's not what our kids need. We know that's not what's best for them. And so as parents, we need to find the time and the energy to step in and find ways to help our kids love reading. We can read to them, talk to them about what they're reading and make time for this by turning off the TV ourselves.* (my emphasis)

This does not require my analysis, because I am reproducing them only to give the readers a food for thought and will like to leave them with this. Mr. Obama's speech on reading can be utilized to project the need for promoting reading as an essential tool for socio-economic transformation of contemporary societies, to project the agenda of reading right into the forefront of social concerns. I am sure, many readers would be more well-informed about what Mr. Obama did or did not do to promote reading preparedness of his people during his Presidency, but that is not the point of debate for me right now because I do not hold any brief for him nor intend to!

This is a slightly revised version of an article written by the author for his blog to coincide with the inauguration of the second term of Mr. Barack Obama as the president of USA in January 2013.

LITERARY ESSAYS

CHAPTER 8

NATION-BUILDING AND DYNAMICS OF TRANSLATION

An Essay in Two Parts

Preface to Both Parts

The present discussion is not intended to be a history of nationalism or history of translation in India. It is presumed that the reader will have basic background of the various forces at work that played their part in the making of India's national identity. By first giving a background into the origins of nation-building process in Europe and coming to the multi-cultural and multi-lingual scenario of India trying to forge a national identity of its own in the aftermath of its encounters with the Empire, the last section, the main part of the discussion, tries to find out various motivations, motifs and under currents of India's socio-cultural reality impacting on the dynamics of translation.

Major turning points, new emerging dialectics at a given period in India's modern history have been discussed with the purpose of analysis and understanding with special emphasis on 19th century which set the tone for future linguistic, textual and cultural dialogues in India. The basic structure of the discussion in the last section hinges on the presentation of translators as discoverers and interpreters. As it happened during the course of the movement of India's socio-cultural and political churning, the lines between translators and interpreters of texts and ideas many a time got blurred and both impacted each other in a crucial manner. Hence dynamics of translation has got to take into account the dynamics of interpretation of cultures, policies and canons and the present discussion approaches the topic from that perspective too.

PART-I

The European Experience

Nation, Nationalism and Nation-Building

The European Experience

The idea of 'Nation-Building' is intrinsically linked to the idea of nation-state and nationalism. A R Desai states:

> Before national communities, national societies, national states, and national cultures came into existence, communities in various parts of the world *generally* lived through tribal, slave, and feudal phases of social existence. At a certain stage of social, economic, and cultural development, nations came into being.........from the sixteenth century onward, national communities, in different stages of national consolidation, have appeared in the amphitheatre of human history'.[1]

Desai quotes E. H. Carr[2] to underline the 'traits that distinguish a nation from a non-national community'. This definition of E. H. Carr, even though Euro-centric and posing some problems for defining India as a nation in these terms, which we will encounter and discuss later, is nevertheless significant from Indian perspective. It underlines that 'nation' is primarily a cultural idea that, however, gets concretized only if it has one political and territorial structure making it a 'state'. Political scientists like Heywood[3] have argued that the boundaries of nation and state should, as far as possible, coincide for a particular geographical, political and cultural region to claim a sovereign nationality of its own. In this sense, nation-states, which emerge out of a sense of nationalism and nation-building and further give impetus to this process, are, as Subhash Kashyap underlines:

> a relatively recent phenomenon. The concept took shape in Europe and the U.K and France emerged as the first nation-states followed by Italy and Germany as late as in the nineteenth century only.[4]

However, some recent studies undertaken from the sociological perspectives and interpretation of the construction of nationalism raise quite valuable questions thus heightening our understanding of the historical evolution of the concept of nation-state and nationalism in modern times. In an important study, G. Aloysius problematises the issues in order to relate the post-nation phase of a society with its pre-nation stage so that the dynamics of changing relationship between culture and power, the two integral aspects of human societies, can be recognized and understood in a proper perspective. Aloysius states:

> If congruence between culture and power is what nation and nationalism is all about, was culture apolitical in the pre-nation or pre-modern stage? While scholarship is divided on this point, the idea

> that culture resents being ruled over by another culture but seeks to set up its own power, is not entirely modern. Certain forms of fusion between culture and power could be identified even in ancient time.[5] In the modern phenomenon of nation a particular form of congruence between culture and power as transition and social change is being indicated.... Nationalism seeks to move away from the notion of the past or pre-modern form of the culture-power fusion, usually unequal, hierarchical, and ascriptive, and construct an equal and homogenous one. The demand of nationalism here, is for equal spread of power over culture as the transition to nation... The nationalist process of politicization in modernity takes hold of culture in its totality, empowering all its members with equal rights and responsibilities, and sets them apart from cultures and individuals outside it.... The masses of men and women who were hitherto excluded from the arena of political power through ascriptive hierarchical structures of privileges/liabilities in society and dynastic rule in polity, now emerge politically in nationalism to constitute the new politico-civil society of equal rights and liabilities. Such is the specific form of congruence between culture and power in modern nationalism.[6]

Constitutionalism and Nation-Building

This aspect of nationalism as constituting a 'new politico-civil society of equal rights and liabilities', brings us to the idea of constitutional reforms as seen in European nation-states as an intrinsic part of the process of nation-building. It is important to note that the process of the coming of nation-states in European countries is marked not only by the unification of various regions of particular cultural and political communities into nation-states; but a simultaneous re-engineering of the legislative, judicial and other political apparatus of the state based on the principles of democracy, equality and individual freedom also define it.

The cumulative effect of the defining social, cultural and political revolutions of the West following the Renaissance and the religious reforms of the 14th-16th centuries, mainly, The Puritan Revolution (1642), The Restoration (1660) and The Glorious Revolution (1688) of England, the American War of Independence (1776), the French Revolution of 1789, The Industrial Revolution starting in mid-18th century etc. is seen in the rising sense of nationalism among the newly emerging nation-states of Europe. Constitutional framework providing one rule of law, one flag, one national anthem, one army underlining political sovereignty, among others, separates the nation-building process of this period with that of the previous ages, which despite best of the intentions and endeavours of the ruling monarchy of the time made it as something non-participative and lacking in national consensus as well as consciousness.

In this context, as a way of illustration and as a representative of the efforts to build a society under a monarchy, one would do well to refer to the great efforts of the Russian monarch, Peter the Great (1689–1725). His thirty-six years of reign is considered epoch making for his sustained and personal touch to all the aspects of national life with his special urge to 'Europeanise' Russia. Hazen gives a graphic and dramatic detail of what Peter, the founder of the great city of St. Petersburg, tried to achieve for Russia in the last decade of the 17th century and the first two decades of the 18th century:

> ...he had sent fifty young Russians of the best families to England, Holland, and Venice to learn the arts and sciences of the West, especially shipbuilding and fortifications. *Later he had gone himself for the same purpose, to study on the spot the civilization whose superiority he recognized and intended to impose upon his own country, if that were possible.* This was a famous voyage. Travelling under the strictest incognito, as 'Peter Mikailovitch', he donned labourer's clothes and

> worked for months in the shipyards of Holland and England. He was interested in everything. He visited mills and factories of every kind, asking innumerable questions: "What is this for? How does that work?" He made a sheet of paper with his own hands. During his hours of recreation he visited museums, theatres, hospitals, galleries. He saw printing presses in operation, attended lectures on anatomy, studied surgery a little, and even acquired some proficiency in the humble and useful art of pulling teeth. He brought collections of laws, and models of all sorts of machines, and engaged many officers, mechanics, printers, architects, sailors, and workmen of every kind, to go to Russia to engage in the task of imparting instruction to a nation which, *in Peter's opinion,* needed it and should receive it, willy nilly.[7]

In the above paragraph, the lines in italics are indeed the best example of nation-building exercise in any society and what we may mean by it. However, the second line of the above paragraph and the words— *in Peter's opinion*—in the last line (highlighted in *italics*) take the sheen, as it were, out of these great efforts of Peter the Great to build Russia, because they do not conform to the questioning of the so-called divine rights of the monarchy to rule over a society in a manner that they deemed fit that the modern nation-states brought about through their internal and intense social, cultural and political debates.

It is typical of the rise of nationalism in European nations in the later half of 18th century and through the 19th century that the efforts for nation-building was also driven by the urge to make the nation people-centric, as something away from it being monarchy-centric, a point that is given its theoretic structure by Aloysius. In Italy, the leaders like Joseph Mazzini (1805–1872) and Giuseppe Garibaldi (1807–1882), while fighting for freedom of Italy, first from the French rule and finally from Austrian control, made the establishment of a free, independent, and republican Italy as integral to their nation-building exercise. On the other hand, when a leader like Otto von Bismarck-Schonhausen (1815–1898) in Germany did not show much regard for making the unification and nation-building exercise in Germany people-centric in true terms, they had to contend with the rise of a Socialist movement in the newly independent nation-state of Germany, leading finally to the establishment of a constitutionally and democratically elected system of governance as the final achievement of the nation-building exercise there.

Similarly, the history of modern France in the 18th and 19th centuries is synonymous with the establishment of various Republics and constitution making process to arrive at the right kind of people-centric political system to mark, as well as, sustain the nation-building exercise. Finally, in England, a constitutional monarchy, the first among the European nations to embrace democracy, wide-ranging reforms were made as a response to the ills, as well as, benefits of the Industrial Revolution during the 18th century and throughout the 19th century. Moreover, the post-Restoration period in England from the latter half of 17th century itself, the English sense of social, political and cultural morality underwent paradigm shift from the pre-Restoration and Elizabethan periods. To quote Hazen:

> ...it was a period of numerous and important changes in the national life. Parliament had been made more representative of the people, the suffrage had been greatly extended, and much economic legislation had been passed, designed to improve the condition of the labouring classes.[8]

It needs to be pointed out that the people-centric constitution also integrally implied separation of religion from the state, though through a long drawn out and complex process, thus bringing in an objective and rule-based state with the intention to serve all without any discrimination based on class, religion, race and gender. In this regard, Shibani Kinkar Chaube makes a valid point:

> A significant point about constitutionalism is that a constitution does not fall from the blue. It is not God-given. Nor is it granted by a benevolent ruler, because no ruler would like to reduce his own power. A constitution is framed by the will of the people or wrested from a ruler; it grows out of the experience and the aspirations of a people.[9]

It is this spirit that finds its fullest expression in the making of the nation-states of Europe in the 18th and 19th centuries, their nationalism and nation-building processes.

Interplay of State Cultural Institutions and Translators in Creating National Identity: Illustration from England

However, we would be missing an important ingredient of the nation-building process as a democratic exercise if we do not take into account the alternative ideologies, the criticism, evaluation and reflection on the mainstream process that are offered by the social, cultural, literary and political thinkers and critics of a particular society as without them no modern and self-analyzing system could be put in place. Creation of public opinion and public understanding of the nation-building process contribute as much to the process itself as the efforts of the State. Moreover, like the social and political consolidation, 'consolidation' in terms of standardization of language and grammar, creation and understanding of individual and community identities through literary and other works, creation of a world view based on local or native perceptions are parallel, integral and inevitable aspects of a genuine nation-building exercise in the modern times where the dynamics of translation willy-nilly plays an important and far reaching role than can be understood apparently.

As a way of illustration and for understanding of the process in the Indian context in the latter part of this discussion, we can go back to the nation-building process that started in England in the mid-seventeenth century and the role that cultural and literary discourse played particularly in the light of nation-building in England in the post-Restoration (1660) period, the period which is historically known for the political and religious upheavals. This heralded the dawn of the 'Modern Age', and the socio-political changes that have parallel and equally revolutionary, as well as, nationalistic stirrings in the making of English language and literature. Legouis and Cazamian put this in a proper perspective:

> From the political point of view the modern development of the English people dates from 1688, but in the moral and literary order the date is 1660....From now onwards, the era of too lofty ambitions and of juvenile errors is closed. Empiricism, in which is summed up the most characteristic genius of the English people, becomes the conscious law governing its existence... A new society and a new literature begin in 1660...The Restoration coincides with one of the most notable changes in the inner being of the English soul.[10]

It may be said that in the post-Restoration period, the English society got down to the job of nation-building process in a scientific and methodical fashion. The Romantic urge of the Renaissance with the Metaphysical poet John Donne (1572–1631), hailing the 'New Philosophy, which doubts all existent beliefs', gave way to the sober, pragmatic, empirical and anti-utopian ideas of the philosophers like John Locke (1632–1704).

It is the period when state established institutions and individual creative thinkers work in tandem, sometimes consciously and sometimes unconsciously, in nation-building processes. Here the examples of Royal Society and the contribution of John Dryden are given to represent all such endeavours that happened in various parts of Europe to contribute to, and to consolidate the construction of, a national identity in the modern times.

An institution like Royal Society, in existence in an informal manner since 1645 and finally receiving its charter incorporated as the Royal Society in 1662, brings in a formal and practical approach to knowledge creation from the nationalistic perspectives in the post-Restoration modern England. The objectives of the Royal Society that are quoted by David Daiches read like a well-laid out architectural plan for social, cultural and intellectual re-construction:

> (The Royal Society) had for its primary purpose the carrying out of practical scientific experiments; its various committees were concerned with mathematics, astronomy, optics, chemistry, agriculture, among other subjects, and it was concerned also with such matters as trade, geography, shipbuilding, architecture, hydraulics, and history. The Society's Philosophical Transactions first began to appear in 1665, with the object of making public "undertakings, studies and labours of the ingenious in many considerable parts of the world."[11]

The Society demanded from its members:

> a close, naked, natural way of speaking, positive expressions, clear senses, a native easiness, bringing as near the mathematical plainness as they can, and preferring the language of artisans, countrymen and merchants before that of wits or scholars...Scientist, Cavalier, citizen and professional writer met in the Royal Society, in whose proceedings Charles II took an interest and whose members included

not only Robert Boyle and Issac Newton but also John Dryden, John Evelyn and Samuel Pepys.[12]

The influence of the Royal Society's dictum for simplicity and clearness in the making of the modern English prose has been acknowledged far and wide by historians with David Daiches proclaiming

> Nobody could now discuss scientific or philosophic topics in the style of Sir Thomas Browne, and Bishop Sprat's History of the Royal Society (1667) both exemplified and recommended a plainer prose style which is seen, in different ways, in Cowley's essays, in the miscellaneous writings of George Savile, Marquis of Halifax (1633–95), in the sermons of Archbishop Tillotson (1630–94), and in Dryden's essays.[13]

The role of the Royal Society may be seen as the earliest form of nation-building to give a shape and direction to national discourse on a variety of issues through state intervention. The idea of simplicity and use of familiar language as propounded by the Royal Society seems to have loomed large on the minds of the translators too.

In this background, the role and contribution of John Dryden (1631–1700), perhaps the best representative of the 'notable changes in the inner being of the English soul', to lift the phrase from Legouis and Cazamian, towards creation and expression of the national temperament of England of the time in his use of themes, idiom and intentions through a large body of his works consisting of poetry, plays, criticism, translations etc is historic. Before we look at his approaches to translation of texts, it is instructive to take a look at his criticism that anticipates a native perspective in his works including translations.

How the national urge to find its own identity and cultural and literary space can directly influence the choice of themes for literary discourse is exemplified through the immediate cause that led to the writing of Dryden's most significant critical piece *An Essay of Dramatic Poesy* (1668). William K Wimsatt Jr. and Cleanth Brooks underline how a French writer Samuel Sorbière's *Voyages* (1663), wherein he made 'highly uncomplimentary remarks about English science and about the English stage'[14], first provoked a reply from the historian of the Royal Society, Thomas Sprat, and later led to the writing of *An Essay of Dramatic Poesy* by Dryden. The following opening lines of the preliminary note 'To the Reader' clearly state the nationalistic motives of writing what is primarily a literary and critical discussion:

> The drift of the ensuing Discourse was chiefly to vindicate the honour of our English Writers, from the censure of those who unjustly prefer the French before them.[15]

In this *Essay*, in the form of a character called Neander, the 'new man', Dryden defends the English against the French stating that 'liveliness' of the English poetry is better than 'cold formality' of the French. The entire *Essay*, so far as Dryden speaks through Neander, presents, in the words of Wimsatt and Brooks 'the dearest moments in the history of national self-appreciation'[16] as he puts the greatest English dramatists such as Shakespeare, Beaumont and Fletcher and Ben Jonson on the highest pedestal of literary genius comparing them with classical poets. To quote from the *Essay*:

> Shakespeare was the Homer, or father of our dramatic poets; Jonson was the Virgil, the pattern of elaborate writing; I admire him, but I love Shakespeare.

One may say that when Dryden, a Classicist, leans towards Shakespeare rather than Jonson, a Classicist in his training and approach, he may as well be merging his voice with the general national perception of Shakespeare being more easily understood and popular among the theatre going public. Considering the immediate provocation as well as the objectives of *An Essay of Dramatic Poesy*, which come from the poet's urge to put the records straight about the literary accomplishments of the major dramatists of England vis-à-vis those of France—'to vindicate the honour of our English Writers'—the *Essay* retains a unique position in the cultural and political dialogue of the country.

This nationalistic spirit works also in Dryden's translations. In 1694 he produced his most ambitious and defining work as translator, *The Works of Virgil* (1697), which was published by subscription. The publication of the translation of Virgil was a national event, for Dryden utilised the translation as a vehicle for contemporary political criticism. Dryden's translation of Virgil's *Aenied* was extensively excerpted in commonplace books of poetry that shaped eighteenth century literary tastes.

As a corollary to this subtle dynamics, the interplay of the individual's creative works with his social or national obligations seems to be one of the reasons why during the last stage of his career Dryden turned to Chaucer for translating his works into modern English. In his *Preface to Fables*, published in the year of his death in 1700, which contain translations of Chaucer along with those of the Italian poet Boccaccio, Dryden places Chaucer in the league of the best of classical poets that also seem to be driven by nationalistic emotions:

> In the first place, As he is the Father of English Poetry, so I hold him in the same Degree of Veneration as the Grecians held Homer, or the Romans Virgil: He is a perpetual Fountain of good Sense; learned in all Sciences; and therefore speaks properly on all Subjects: As he knew what to say, so he knows also when to leave off; a

> Continence which is practised by few Writers, and scarcely by any of the Ancients, excepting Virgil and Horace.[17]

For a poet, who found ways to create better understanding about the works of the classical writers like Homer, Virgil, Ovid etc. by translating them and adapting them for the contemporary taste driven by the Classicists' belief in the Idea of *Imitation* turning his attention towards Chaucer is no mean historical and literary event of the time as it hinted at rehabilitating a native classical poet as part of the nation-building process. Moreover, as David Daiches observes, Dryden utilized the translations of the classical poets as well as those from Chaucer in order to strengthen the English language, in order to bring in more vitality to a language that needed to acquire an identity of its own and also needed to come out of the shadows of the Italian and French languages besides the classical sources of Latin and Greek. Talking about the translations collected in the *Fables*, Daiches states:

> Sometimes Dryden imposes a false dignity on his originals by substituting high-sounding generalizations for clearly realized particulars. His Fables…contain his renderings from Chaucer and Boccaccio, and this includes some of his most vigorous narrative, though even here his tendency to heighten the language, to give a rhetorical gloss to a simple statement, is often in evidence.[18]

Actually, in the great post-Restoration debate between the modern and classical, between native and foreign, Dryden somehow could always strike a balance, and despite his Classical and high Augustan training, could, many a time, lean towards that which was familiar and home-grown—a reflection of Reason based on one's own socio-cultural context. In this context, Mona Baker and Gabriela Saldanha make an observation that better analyses

Dryden's role as a great interpreter and translator negotiating, and making bridges, with the classical and modern literary periods of Europe at a particular historical moment of England, thereby providing it a national framework for further literary explorations. To quote:

> Dryden's works shows how a web of translation practices combines both 'domesticating' and 'foreignising' elements and how categorizations of these can shift. He used previous translations, absorbed the language of his predecessors Spenser, Shakespeare and Milton, itself already classicized (Haynes 2003), and in turn influenced practice and aesthetics in both translation and literature making the boundaries between the two more porous.[19]

In this sense, he is the true representative of the post-Restoration age, 'which', as Legouis and Cazamian point out, 'determines itself with relation to that which precedes it…But in all other respects, it is towards the future that it tends.'[17] T S Eliot makes a perceptive comment that not only corroborates Samuel Johnson's remark about Dryden being 'the Father of English Criticism' but also underlines his contribution to the understanding, making and expression of the English identity. Eliot states:

> The great work of Dryden in criticism is that at the right moment he became conscious of the necessity of affirming the native element in literature. Dryden is more consciously English, in his plays, than were his predecessors; his essays on the drama and on the art of translation are conscious studies of the nature of English theatre and the English language; and even his adaptation of Chaucer is an assertion of the native tradition rather than what it has sometimes been taken to be, an amusing and pathetic failure to appreciate the beauty of the Chaucerian language and metric. Where the Elizabethan critics for the most part, were aware of something to be borrowed

> or adapted from abroad, Dryden was aware of something to be preserved at home.[21]

Hence when Samuel Johnson stated about Dryden that he found English language 'brick and left it marble', Johnson is not only paying a tribute to the genius of Dryden but also clearly underlining his contribution to the process of nation-building of which the maturing of English language is a powerful and integral element. Dryden, through his approach, made England realize that while Shakespeare was the father of dramatic poets in the country, Chaucer was the father of English poetry, thereby himself becoming the father of English criticism and prose. This finding of father-figures in various fields of enquiry has been an integral aspect of nationalism in its earliest phases and Dryden in his own way discovers as well as becomes such patriarchal requirements of nation-building. In this sense, Dryden proves to be the precursor of that long list of poets, writers, thinkers, critics and translators like Alexander Pope, Samuel Johnson, William Blake, S T Coleridge, William Wordsworth, Shelley, Tennyson, Dickens, Carlyle etc. who provided through their works a critique as well as direction to the various strands that have gone into the making of England as a modern nation-state while also acting as father-figures of English literary movement in different periods.[22]

However, when we come to the Indian context in the next part of this essay we will realize that the nation-building process here differs from the European experience in two very crucial way: a) the multi-lingual and multi-cultural set up of India, and b) the strange colonial experience that the country had to undergo. Both required a constant need for interpreters who could define, re-define and come to terms with a national identity.

CHAPTER 9

NATION-BUILDING AND DYNAMICS OF TRANSLATION

PART-II
THE INDIAN CONTEXT

Nation-Building in India

Idea and Perception

It is indeed one of the ironies of history that during the period of 17th, 18th and 19th centuries when most nations of Europe were undergoing upheaval for progressive changes in their respective societies, many of them, most prominently England and France, were also simultaneously intensely engaged in spreading the tentacles of colonialism in the countries of Asia, Africa and Latin America. In fact, colonialism was the other and darker face of the rise of nationalism among the European nation-states. While they fought to make their own societies just, equal and based on freedom of thought, during the same period they justified their growing colonial power in other continents on the grounds of trade and religion ultimately taking the form of intellectual and cultural superiority sustained through their political and military might and economic exploitation. It is a telling historical fact that the East India Company that was granted a Royal Charter and the exclusive privilege to trade in the East by Queen Elizabeth (1558–1603) on 31st December 1600, 'was from the beginning linked with the monarchy with the Queen herself being one of the shareholders of the Company'.[1]

As a matter of fact, the entry of the European forces into India, in particular, and into the countries of Asia and Africa, in general, during the 15th–17th centuries led by the Portuguese and the Spanish and followed by the British, Dutch and French was the direct impact of the battle of supremacy that was being played out among these major countries of Europe during the period. As we have seen previously, these European nations were themselves undergoing respective nationalistic catharsis to become modern as well as powerful and in order to sustain their national endeavours, imperialistic expansion was considered a major economic and political policy. J. Pirenne in his *History of the Universe*, published in Paris in 1950 stated:

> In the middle of the seventeenth century, Asia still had a far more important place in the world than Europe...The riches of Asia were incomparably greater than those of the European states. Her industrial techniques showed a subtlety and a tradition that the European handicrafts did not possess. And there was nothing in the more modern methods used by the traders of the Western countries that Asian trade had to envy. In matters of credit, transfer of funds, insurance, and cartels, neither India, Persia, nor China had anything to learn from Europe.[2]

Bipan Chandra underlines the European urge to not imbibe but rather takeover the Asian and Indian advances in trade and commerce to fulfil its own imperialistic as well as respective national needs:

> In fact, at the dawn of the 18th century, India was one of the main centres of world trade and industry. Peter the Great of Russia was led to exclaim:
>
> > *Bear in mind that the commerce of India is the commerce of the world and…he who can exclusively command it is the dictator of Europe.*[3]

Considering the upheaval of Europe and the great social, political, economic and cultural consolidation programmes that were going on in its major countries during the period, on the one hand, and the relatively stable, peaceful and rather well-organised life that the Indians had come to acquire under the Mughal Empire, on the other, it appears that the zeal of the former to progress by all means was to provide a body blow to the socio-political, economic and cultural structures of the latter. Due to this interaction, while Europe, especially England, moved to a greater economic, cultural and political pedastal, India, as a colonised state, battled to first find its lost identities which resulted in the creation of new national identities of which colonial mindset would continue to remain a major influencing factor.

However, having said this, in the context of India, though it is true that the ever expanding and imperialist designs of the British colonised the country, it is equally true that the lack of any sense of national culture or national consciousness proved to be the great complementary reason for the eastablishment as well as sustenance of the colonial rule in the country. Analysing India's first war of independence of 1857 which erupted quite late, and its failure due to lack of unity among various sections of the country—the peasants, the zamindars, the Princely rulers, the educated Indians etc.— Bipan Chandra states:

> The lack of unity among Indians was perhaps unavoidable at this stage of Indian history. Modern nationalism was yet unknown in India. Patriotism meant love of one's small locality or region or at most one's state. Common all-India interests and the consciousness that these interests bound all Indians together were yet to come.[4]

But this national consciousness, the first integral basis as well as part and parcel of nation-building exercise, in the colonial India came into being through a very intricate process which is all reflected in the social, political, cultural, intellectual and economic thought of the period impacting on the dynamics of translation works of the period. This process of the growth of nationalism is put very succintly by A R Desai in the following words:

> The growth of nationalism in India was an uneven process, both regarding tempo and time, among different communities and provinces…nationalism grew in India as a result of the conditions created by the British conquest and rule and the action of the forces accompanying this conquest and rule. Since this conquest as well as the penetration of new forces did not take place throughout the country at the same time, the conditions, which led to the rise of political and national consciousness, matured unevenly among different parts and communities.[5]

It is no wonder then that despite what India as a politically free, independent and sovereign nation could achieve by organising one national identity for itself through constitutionalism, it is frequently debated whether it really has a uniform identity applicable to all regions, language communities and the like. Eminent linguist Gopal Haldar poses and analyses this national dilemma rather directly:

> Is India a nation, or is it a super-nation or a union of nations? For, the Indian Union, or the India that is Bhārat is not merely a community as defined in anthropological terms; nor is it a nation as described in political terms. We shall … assume India to be a super-nation; and we shall accept the states included in it as being individual nation-like bodies.[6]

Gopal Haldar's analysis appears to be more in the nature of a self-dialogue because despite the complexities that India as a civilization vs. India as a modern nation-state debate offer, the achievement of the latter has mesmerized the global community. The post-independent India and the manner in which it has been able to put into practice the idea of 'unity in diversity' through a successful model of multi-party democracy, secularism addressing the needs and aspirations of the multi-lingual and multi-cultural communities, has been viewed with awe and admiration especially among the newly created nation-states of Asia and Africa. What the then President Chandrika Bandaranaike Kumaratunga of Sri Lanka stated in a candid speech can be taken as a representative perception about India's successful nation-building endeavours:

> You have in India made a serious attempt at building a pluralist and non-sectarian society since Independence. The Constitution of India intrinsically recognises the diversity of the numerous ethno-religious and cultural groups of peoples living in India while according to them the legal and political authority to maintain that diversity within the united, yet federal state of India. We know that this is the strength of modern India, which by any definition is not simply a country but almost a whole sub-continent. India has managed to cope with the myriad diversities within it while maintaining a sufficiently stable political system. It continues to be one of the world's most vibrant democracies. The uprisings that occur and the

> rumblings that one hears from some of the numerous communities living in the federal state of India are perhaps caused by some delays in implementing the rights and privileges given to each one of those groups by the Constitution.
>
> In Sri Lanka we have faltered in the essential task of nation-building since Independence. With much less diversity of race, religion and language than you have, we have failed to address the issue of building a truly pluralist nation state.[7]

Understandably Gopal Haldhar also agrees

> Despite being a single nation, India is a land of many languages and many races in its size and its population. It is said that its size is comparable to that of Continental Europe. If one keeps in mind how many countries there are, how many languages spoken, how many nation-states have evolved and how many differences and at various points in time battles and wars have occurred amongst them on the European landmass, the complexities of national integration in India do not appear surprising at all. Instead, the extent of unity that has grown within it is an especially surprising fact of history. One just has to remember, though, that this trend in history, having continued slowly so far, has not yet reached completion.[8]

Nation-Building and Dynamics of Translation in India

In this backdrop, where Indian nationalism has been seen as something that developed much later in the day and 'as a result of the conditions created by the British conquest and rule and the action of the forces accompanying this conquest and rule', on the one hand, and still unable to strictly fit in the concept of European nation-state, though attracting admiration for its achievements in integrating the nation as a political and cultural entity, on the other, we can identify various dynamics that impact and motivate the translation works. These dynamics are very typically linked with 'discoveries' —and interpretations of such discoveries, which is integral and natural corollary— on multi-dimensional planes and leave their mark on various phases of nation-building process in modern India including the earliest stages of colonialism, its consolidation, anti-colonialism, and post-colonialism. Aloysius talks about the internal and external forces which a society has to struggle and come to terms with to find its desired sense of nationalism. According to him:

> The external reference is to other cultures, nations and nation-states, which are perceived as obstacles in the way of one's own nationalism. This obstacle need not always be actual control by another culture as under imperialism, but could be graded one… The internal dimension of the culture-power fusion is what constitutes the specifically modern element in the notion of the nation. Here the reference is to the culture's own past as the other.[9]

Broadly speaking, in Indian context, the following three patterns of 'discoveries'—which are in response to external, internal and quasi-external and quasi-internal dynamism— can be identified which have motivated translation activities and contributed to nation-building:

1 'Discovery of India' by the Europeans and the Indians: *Translations with Religious, Cultural, Linguistic and Political Motivations*
2. Discovery of Europe and the Larger World by the Indians under Colonialism: *Translation of Texts and Ideas*
3. Discovery of the New and Suppressed Identities by the Indians: *Translation for Linguistic, Textual, Social, Cultural, Political and Gender Identities*

It would be appropriate to state that these discoveries are related to each other as well as isolated, they influence each other and remain untouched too, they work in tandem as well as at cross-purposes, and they exist sometimes in similar time and space and sometimes follow or precede each other at different spaces. But these discoveries stem from the basic guiding principle of the translator as discoverer and interpreter who finds ways to underline connection as well as disconnection between two or more periods, texts, ideas, languages and cultures. The basic textual and contextual issues of translation studies—who is the translator, what does he or she translate, in what circumstances, from what to which language, and why does the translation take place—are connected to each other so closely that it would be instructive to discuss these discoveries concurrently as far as possible to understand the process of the evolution of India as a modern nation-state impacting upon the changing dialectics of the translation of texts and ideas. It needs to be underlined that due to the unique and tortuous process of colonialism through which India came to be a modern nation-state, the dynamics of translation are not only about translation and interpretation of actual text, written or oral, but, more importantly, it is about discovery and interpretation of cultures, religions, classes, languages, identities, policies and canons.

Hence, though the concept of Nation-Building is generally seen from the perspective of the clashes and interactions that took place between India as a colonized nation and England as the Colonial power which started to make their impact from the second half of the 18th century, a grounding in the earliest explorations and experiments done by the European missionaries from Portugal, Dutch, Denmark, Germany etc starting from the second half of the 16th century and running through the 17th and ultimately merging with the experiments of the British colonial policies related to Indian culture and society would be in order to have a historical perspective of this dynamics.

Translation as Discovery

Between Vasco De Gama's 'discovery' of India through the discovery of a new sea route from Portugal to India via Cape of Good Hope in 1498 and Jawaharlal Nehru's work *Discovery of India* published in 1946, we can place the two levels of discoveries about Indian culture and civilization that happened during the periods 16th-20th centuries as far as Indian contact with the modern European world is concerned —one at the hands of the Europeans and another at the hands of Indians themselves. For the Europeans, the emphasis should fall on 'discovery' per se of India as India was always there though unknown to a part of Europe at a particular period of history. However, for the Indians, it is the discovery of the fabled lost glory of the ancient past, of its own living languages and cultures, its own contradictions and inequalities in its social, cultural, linguistic and economic structures and a national consciousness about the idea of India as a political entity that marks such a discovery, hence the emphasis is more on 'India'.

Earliest Explorations in the South India

In the 16th and 17th centuries, when the Mughal Empire was at its pinnacle, a quiet experiment with far reaching consequences was being conducted by the travelers and missionaries from different parts of Europe following on the sea route discovered for them by Vasco da Gama. For the purpose of present discussion, we can refer to the translation of the Bible and other Christian materials into Indian languages, introduction of printing press and moveable types in the South Indian coastal centers of Goa, Kerala and Tamil Nadu as part of these experiments. The basic motive behind the discovery of sea routes to India and other parts of Asia by the early Europeans was two-fold: 'trade opportunities and reclamation of new worlds to the Christian faith.'[10]

These missionaries, deputed by the royal courts of Portugal, Dutch, Denmark, Germany, France, England, Spain etc, were quick to understand the multi-lingual scenario of India and learned Indian languages, especially Sanskrit, prepared grammars of various Indian languages, compiled dictionaries and introduced a scientific framework for translation and understanding of Indian 'market'. The first such efforts were made by the Portuguese and the languages that came in for this historically significant religio-linguistic experiments first in India were Tamil and Thamizh, though the former having larger base saw publication of more works.

Reference to the printing of *Cartilha*, a Portuguese primer on Christian psalms and hymns, in Tamil language with Roman script at Lisbon as early as in 1554 is found.[11] Gradually, as the printing presses started getting set up from the later half of 16th century onwards, we find printing of Christian texts as well as Indian language dictionaries and grammar in Tamil, Konkani, Goan etc taking place in India itself, first in Roman script and later with the development of the moveable types, in the original scripts of these languages themselves. Kesavan records the printing of series of works like Tamil *Catechism* (1577), *Doctrina Christina* in Tamil (1578 and 1579), Tamil *Confessionary* (1580)-all translated from Portuguese as the earliest efforts of the Portuguese missionaries to propagate the 'Word of God' among the Indian people.

However, it is a misnomer to say that the efforts of the Christian missionaries of Europe to translate Christian religious texts in Indian languages were all happening in harmony among themselves. The schism between the Catholics and Protestants, the contradictions arising out of national identities as most of the missionaries were sponsored by their monarchies and had to report back to them about their work in India for further sustenance, and finally impediments put forth by the trading companies like various East Indian Companies of different countries to the work of the missionaries of their countries out of the fear that the religious conversions would affect their trade and commerce and out of the suspicion that the missionaries would report to the rulers their corrupt practices in India—all this created a spirit of literary and personal rivalry that gets reflected in the translation works done by the travelers and missionaries in the 17th and 18th centuries. While the conservatives learnt Indian languages to translate only the Christian texts in these languages and also maintained social distance in India, mention[12] of the Italian missionary Robert de Nobili (1577–1656) for showing the path of social as well as linguistic assimilation is made. Living like a Hindu saint, he is said to be one of the earliest to translate the four Vedas into French.

However, the Protestant missionaries like the famous Danish Bartholomew Ziegenbalg (1688–1719), who worked at the Danish settlement Tranquebar in Kerala, not only mingled with the Tamil culture and language but also tried to connect with the people. His Tamil translations of *New Testament* and the *Apostles* were done after years of learning Tamil language with native Tamil scholars. This translation is supposed to be livelier and more authentic and William Carey's successes later on took a lot from Ziegenbalg's works.[13] Ziegenbalg, in his letters also criticized the 'sinister Practices and Underhand Dealings' of the Catholic missionaries thus setting the stage 'for an implicit and at times overt antagonism between Catholic and Protestant.'[14] This interplay of impressing upon the Indian people to embrace Christianity, on the one hand, and criticizing similar work of missionaries belonging to different sects and nations, on the other, present a complex pattern of the fusion of culture and power in the early phases of the 'discovery of India' by the European missionaries.

The Italian Jesuit Priest Rev. Beschi (d. 1746) is another example of one who tried to communicate closely with the Indian populace but at the same time distanced himself from other missionaries. As an accomplished Tamil scholar, he wrote the Tamil epic *Tempavani*, commemorating the glory of St. Joseph, thus starting the process of translation of idea, rather than the text from the West directly into Indian languages. However, at the same time, he was sustained in his 'diatribes against the Danish Mission of Tranquebar.'[15] He criticized Ziegenbalg's Tamil translation of *New Testament* thus:

> Already on reading the first line the reader's eyes burn, his tongue dried up and his ears must burst. One looks around and burst into loud laughter.[16]

However, the inspiration that these early endeavours of the missionaries gave 'did not fall upon fertile soil'[17] and their works remained largely confined among the scholars and in the European libraries as rare manuscripts and books. But there was no doubt that their works had achieved, first, a lasting perception about the crucial role that translations would play in India for spreading religion, trade and ultimately the structures of the Empire, and secondly, on more concrete level, the compiling of grammars, bi-lingual dictionaries of Indian languages with many European languages and the development of printing processes.

Emergence of British Raj and Explorations in and from Bengal

The decisive Battle of Plassey fought in 1757 in the aftermath of the swift decline of the Mughal empire following the death of Aurangzeb in 1707, established British supremacy in Bengal eventually leading to the extension of the same across Indian regions like the Marathas, Hyderabad, Mysore, Avadh, Punjab etc in the next 50 years or so. The period also saw final decimation by the British of the French imperialistic ambitions in India thereby making them the sole claimant of the resources of this vast territory called India. During this period, the British East India Company's administration of India now came to be directly regulated by the British government through various parliamentary acts like the Regulating Act (1773), Pitts' India Act (1784) and by the Charter Act of 1833, 'the trade monopoly of the Company in India was ended and trade with India was thrown open to all British subjects.'[18]

With long presence in India, first as trader and now as proper colonizer, and with various experiments by Christian missionaries during the last two centuries in South India as discussed above, and ultimately reaching Bengal and other parts of the country—willy-nilly the stage now seemed set for institutional intervention by the British for introduction of English and Western education which would have far reaching impact on India as a cultural and political entity, even though the British were not aware of the existence of the experiments of the Christian missionaries in the South India.[19] At the dawn of the 19th century they systematically worked on two simultaneous planes to consolidate and sustain their colonial rule in India: by draining India's wealth and diverting the same to their own country by introducing suitable changes in land ownership and revenue generation system and secondly by expanding administrative apparatus like the railways, roads and the postal & telecommunication services across India over a period of time. The introduction and spread of the western education was designed to impart a cultural and ideological framework to these policies and to impregnate the Indian society with the idea of cultural superiority of the West through creation of a class of professionals like lawyers, doctors, teachers, journalists, judges, officers etc and this served the British Raj well so far as it could.

However, along with the practical needs of the Empire to introduce Indian language learning and translations from and into Indian languages of a variety of texts, a Romantic approach of the Western scholars not directly connected with the British Empire also played its part in the discovery of India consciousness of the West with translation of ancient Indian texts into Western languages playing a major role of mediator between the colonial masters and the colonized, and the East and the West. In the first category, such work as started under the Governor-General Warren Hastings (1772–1785), whom Percival Spear called the first British administrator 'to understand Indian culture as a basis for sound Indian administration'[20] and later carried on by his successors can be placed which were meant to consolidate the gains of the Empire. Reference to the compilation of a book in Sanskrit based on Indian law books entitled *Vivadarnavasetu* (Bridge to Cross the Ocean of Disputes) and its translation into English via Persian by Nathaniel Brassey Halhed as *A Code of Gentoo Law* (1776) under the guidance of Hastings to help British officials understand the sources of legal administration in India can be made to underline the use of translation for culture-power fusion. Hastings also encouraged the Sanskrit scholar Charles Wilkins to take lessons from the native Sanskrit scholars at Benaras and 'as the first fruit' he published in

1785 an English translation of *Bhagwadgita*, with a foreword by Warren Hastings which was followed by a translation of *Hitopadesa*.[21]

The establishment by the Governor-General Lord Wellesely (1798–1805) of Fort William College at Calcutta 'to teach Indian languages to European functionaries to enable them to govern the country more efficiently' and The Christian Mission at Serampore 'to promote Christianity in Bengal', both in 1800, are examples of the institutionalization of the process. Presided over by scholars, multi-linguists and men of conviction, the former by John Gilchrist (1759–1842) the latter by the trio of William Carey (1761–1834), William Ward (1769–1823) and Joshua Marshman (1769–1834), both the institutions worked in tandem to achieve their objectives. The Serampore Press under Carey printed translations of the Bible in more than 45 languages, of which 38 were translated at Serampore. Carey himself translated wholly or partly in 28 languages, which included a wide range of Indian languages as well as many foreign languages.[22] Similarly, The Fort William College prescribed and published a range of titles in Arabic, Bengali, Hindustani (Hindi and Urdu), Persian, English, Sanskrit etc. However, besides translations of various ancient Sanskrit Hindu religious as well as secular texts, tales from the Arabian world into Indian langauges, a great deal of emphasis was given on books that could teach the students or at best give them a smattering of knowledge about grammar and Indian languages through books prepared in English language with titles like *Arabic Syntex, A Grammar of the Arabic Language, Dialogues Intended to Facilitate the Acquiring of the Bengalee Language, The Strangers' East India Guide to the Hindoostanee, Dialogues: English and Hindoostanee* etc.[23] Later in 1812, the College of Fort St. George was founded at Madras with the similar purpose to act as translator and interpreter of South Indian languages to train the British officials in India. Headed by Francis Whyte Ellis (1777–1819), the college propounded the Dravadian languages as separate family and achieved this by translating some passages from Sanskrit and English into Tamil, Telugu and Kannada and further analyzing the sentence structures of the translated texts.

In the second category, the role of the translation works of the Orientalists, both English as well as other Europeans, led by Asiatic Society of Bengal (1784) founded by William Jones (1746–1794), needs to be seen in the light that they while in crucial ways provided a cultural and intellectual vehicle to consolidate imperialism in its broadest sense, they also at many places cut through the garb of superiority that the colonial masters had taken upon themselves. Patterned on the Royal Society of London, the Asiatic Society's founder was the first man to pronounce the genealogical connection of Sanskrit with Greek and Latin ...and to presume its connection with German, Celtic and Persian.[24] Following on the German missionary Benjamin Schultze, who emphasized the similarity between the *numerals* of Sanskrit, German and Latin'[25], Sir William Jones in 1786 made the following epoch-making observation in his third Annual Discourse on the History and Culture of the Hindus, which in no way matches with the kind of cultural superiority that the British rulers were trying to impose upon India as part of their imperialistic policies:

> The Sanskrit language, whatever be its antiquity, is of a wonderful structure; more perfect than the Greek, more copious than the Latin, and more exquisitely refined than either, yet bearing to both of them a stronger affinity, both in roots of verbs and in the forms of grammar...[26]

William Jones' translation into English of Kaildasa's classical Sanskrit drama *Sakuntala* in 1789 proved to be a historically defining moment in the spread of Orientalism in Germany and other places of Europe. Translated into German by George Forster in 1791, it 'roused the enthusiasm of people like Herder and Goethe.'[27] He also translated into English 'the most respected work of Indian legal literature, the *Law Book of Manu* in 1794, which got translated into German in 1797.[28] The two literary journals of the Asiatic Society, the *Asiatic Miscellany* and the *Asiatic Researches*, regularly published in English translation of the poetry of Persian poets like Hafiz, Durd, Sadi, Hamsaah, Abu Nasiruddin, and also hyms to Hindu gods and goddesses Narayan, Brahma, Vyas, Durga, Bhawani, Prakrati translated from Sanskrit to English.[29] Sir William Jones, as a judge in Supreme Court of Judicature in 1783, also commented on Halhed's translation of *Gentoo Code* finding it not up-to-mark:

> But, whatever be the merit of the original, the translation of it has no authority, and is of no other use than to suggest inquiries on many dark passages, which we find in it: properly speaking, indeed, we can not call it a translation…[30]

At the Asiatic Society, William Jones was succeeded by Henry Thomas Colebrooke who became the real founder of Indian philology and archeology.[31]

The translation of ancient Indian texts into English and through it into various European languages as part of the Orientalist's 'adventure' to discover the 'forgotten and missed' texts of Asia brought about a surge of activities in the form of translations.[32] Wilkins' translation of *Gita* got translated into several European languages like French, German, Italian and Russian. In Germany, the Romantics led by Schlegel brothers, Schopenhauer, Herder and Humboldt and with their enthusiasm shared by the greatest living poet of the time Goethe and later sustained by Max Mueller, heralded the study of ancient Indian texts *Upanishad, Ramayana, Mahabharata, Bhagvadgita,*

Sakuntala, Panchatantra, Manu's Law Book after translating them into German directly from Sanskrit. The last decades of the 18th century and the first half of 19th century thus proved to be the phase of profound philosophical and spiritual discovery of India motivating translation works of the period in the West.

An assessment of the translation works of the Orientalists alongwith those undertaken at the Fort William College and the Serampore Mission would bear out what had been stated above that they supplemented each other in strengthening the cultural part of the Empire and ensuring a foothold for the British in the multi-linguistic and multi-cultural Indian space. The pattern of cultural dialogue created by their works show that the native Indian scholars remained silent partners in these studies. Partha Chatterjee quotes Anour Abdel-Malek to underline how under a dominating framework Orientalism work where the Orient and the Orientals were:

> An 'object' of study, stamped with an otherness—as, all that is different, whether it be 'subject' or 'object'—but of a constitutive otherness, of an essentialist character…This 'object' of study will be, as is customary, passive, non-participative, endowed with a 'historical' subjectivity, above all, non-active, non-autonomous, non-sovereign with regard to itself…[33]

However, in the complex colonial environment, it was natural that the Indians venerated the German Orientalists, who empowered them towards the task of nation-building through the valorization of the Sanskrit language and literature.[34] On the other hand, the works done at Fort William College and Serampore evoked suspicion about their intentions as they certainly smacked of the great imperialist design to establish cultural superiority of England over India and to strengthen its administrative apparatus. Sisir Kumar Das puts it succinctly:

> The orientalists studied the ancient history, and philosophy and literature of India with a zeal comparable to some extent with that of the scholars who studied Greek letters during the renaissance. The scholars who worked in the College of Fort William cannot be compared with the Orientalists at all. The British Orientalist even when they were protagonists of British colonialism succeeded in keeping their scholarly persuasion free from their official duties and colonial interests. The Fort William College, on the other hand, was established primarily to help the British civil servants. Its academic programmes were designed to teach them Indian languages which were useful as tools of administrative efficiency. Its policies were guided not by the scholars interested in Indian culture but mainly by the Directors of the East India Company many of whom had strong aversion to things Indian.[35]

But, when Das states the following in the same piece, we need to take a fresh look at this comparison:

> The kind of exercise the College encouraged, very clearly indicates its interest in the living languages of India and of the adjoining countries, as opposed to the Asiatic Society's which was primarily in the Indian past.[36]

Actually speaking both these endeavours, like all other colonial interventions, first gave some kind of national identity to Indians, who would later discover for themselves how flawed such identities were. The Orientalists' uncritical admiration of India's past, overlooking its colonized and subjugated present, and apparently with no stake in its future, take the sheen out of their scholarly works and image-making about India in the international arena and conform to what Edward W. Said said about Orientalism that it was a 'kind of Western projection onto and will to govern over the Orient.'[37]

On the other hand, the endeavours of the College and the Mission to bring in the study of Indian languages and grammar within the scientific framework broke the elitist mindset of the traditional Indian scholars, albeit by default. When Das makes the following statement in his essay on Halhed, the first to prepare *A Grammar of the Bengal Language* in 1778, in many senses he hits at the root cause of India's colonization:

> ...the Indian scholars, though deeply engrossed with the problems of Sanskrit grammar, and to some extent that of Arabic and Persian hardly felt the necessity for preparing grammars of the living languages around them. There was no pedagogic necessity for a Bengali grammar since Bengali was not *studied* at the higher level. And most probably Bengali scholars did not consider Bengali, a language spoken by the common man, to be a proper subject for scholarly investigation.[38]

In a sense, both the British Orientalists and the cultural and educational institutions under the British Raj made significant discoveries about India and its ancient past as well as living cultures for their own limited purposes fully utilizing the interpretative role of the translation of texts which would make complex and lasting impact on the educated Indians and their desire to have a 'national' identity. However, the 'historic' role that Fort William College played in making forays into the linguistic scene of India and tweaking with the Indian cultural space from their own perspective, is missed when, while making an evaluation of the role of the Fort William College in the context of Urdu, Muhammad Sadiq, takes it all at face value:

> The Fort William College made no original contribution to literature and the works produced there are translations and adaptations... Little indeed has our modern prose been influenced by the Fort

> William College translators that if the college had never existed the course of modern Urdu prose in all probability would not have differed, in any important respect, from what it has been.[39]

Dara Shikoh, Raja Ram Mohun Roy and the Discovery of 'India'

Before we discuss this aspect of the translation works of the 19th century onwards, a word would be in order about the role played by the unfortunate Mughal Prince Dara Shikoh (1615–1659), the Persian and Sanskrit scholar and poet and son of Mughal emperor Shahjahan in, first, providing the source book of the German Orientalism of the 18th century, albeit by default, and secondly underlining a tradition of the discovery of India through translations which would anticipate the contribution of Raja Ram Mohun Roy. Dara Shikoh translated 50 Upanishads from its original Sanskrit into Persian in 1657 under the title *Oupnek'hat* with the help of Sanskrit scholars whom he called to Delhi from Benaras. This was translated by the French scholar Anquetil Duperron from Persian into Latin in 1801–02.[40] Though the quality of the Latin translation was not very good still it was this translation on the basis of which the German Orientalist Schopenhauer (1788– 1860) declared the Upanishad as 'the product of highest human wisdom' setting forth further explorations in Indic studies as discussed above.[41]

Dara Shikoh, as a contemporary of John Dryden and also of the Christian missionaries who first set foot in India and established their connection with this country through translations as discussed above, utilized the unique position of translator as an interpreter of texts and contexts to explore a common mystical language between Islam and Hinduism. His translation endeavour was not motivated from the perpspective of romanticising India's past, but as someone having stakes in the composite fabric of India, he addressed through his translations to the audience of his own country—a role that Raja Ram Mohun Roy (1772–1833) would perform in the changed scenario, though he also had added task of counter-communicating the same to the colonial rulers and Christian missionaries.

A learned scholar who knew over a dozen languages including Sanskrit, Persian, Arabic, English, French, Latin, Greek and Hebrew with knowledge of Sanskrit Literature, Hindu and Jain philosophy, Koran and the Bible[42], among others, Raja Ram Mohun Roy appeared on Indian horizon at the dawn of the 19th century like a foil to the cultural hegemony being consctructed by the British. However, the approach of Roy was not sentimental or romantic, but rational. Hence, even though he defended the traditional Hindu tenets, he also proved to be quite critical of the evil practices and superstitions that had taken the vitality out of them, and championed social and religious reforms. Wintermitz makes a very perceptive comparative study of the intentions of the two contemporaries, Schopenhauer and Roy, in translating and interpretating the Upanishad:

> ...at about the same time when Schopenhauer in Germany was fancying to see his own ideas in the Upanishads of the Hindus rather than deduce them from them...in India...Ram Mohan Roy...found the purest divine faith in the same Upanishads and from the same Upanishads tried to prove to his countrymen that idolatory of the present day Indian religions was to be condemned, yet there was no reason for Indians to accept Christianity; and that they could, if only they understood them, find a pure religion in them.With the intention...that the best of what they (christian theologians and missionaries) taught was already found in the Upanishads, he translated into English a large number of the Upanishads and edited some of them in original text.[43]

How a particular text, Upanishads in the present discussion, can become a site of intellectual, cultural, religious and also political debate across time and space through translations in changing contexts is best exemplified here. In 1815, Roy also translated the *Vedanta Grantha* into Bengali from Sanskrit thus anticipating an altogether new trend of Sanskrit, Persian and later English texts getting translated into modern Indian lanaguges which further resulted in these languages becoming a vehicle of intellectual and social discourse. Through his translations, pamphlets and journals he helped evolve a modern and elegant prose style for Bengali, of which he also compiled a grammar.

The Dilemma of the Discoverers and Interpreters

An integral aspect of the discovery of 'India' by the enlightened Indians was the realisation about the social and religious ills and discriminations present in the Indian society in various implicit and explicit forms- a realisation which would be the leading feature of the construction of national and later sub-national identites. Roy was among the first to underline this and hence the first to face the dilemma of choosing between the fruits of the liberal and rational Western education to achieve socio-cultural reforms in the society and continued inequalities of the Indian society as a way to safeguard its ancient culture and heritage. Roy advocated modern English education for the Indians with learning in Indian culture and heritage. This position of moving forward set the tone of the nation-building endeavours in modern India and no prominent Indian of the 19th and 20th century deviated from this approach.[44] This position taken by Roy and others was used to its advantage by the British. The (in) famous Minutes of Macaulay of 1835 recommended English education for India with an imperialistic pride and arrogance, though spoken within a utilitarian framework:

> …it is impossible for us, with our limited means, to attempt to educate the body of the people. We must at present do our best to form a class who may be interpreters between us and the millions whom we govern, —a class of persons Indian in blood and colour, but English in tastes, in opinions, in morals and in intellect. To that class we may leave it to refine the vernacular dialects of the country, to enrich those dialects with terms of science borrowed from the Western nomenclature, and to render them by degrees fit vehicles for conveying knowledge to the great mass of the population.[45]

Roy, belonging to pre-Macaulay era, would not have completely visualized the full import of having an English education system in so far as it sought to 'create a class of persons Indian in blood and colour, but English in tastes, in opinions, in morals and in intellect'. Though it would take the entire nineteenth century for such a class of interpreters to emerge visibly, 'but a class of such interpreters indeed emerged and the growth of the modern Indian languages was regulated by it. The new literature that developed in all modern Indian languages was a creation of this class.'[46] Moreover, Roy stood at and spoke from a unique historical cusp in Indian cultural history, wherein with a solid background of the two most powerful classical languages of India, Sanskrit and Persian, he had also mastered the new emerging one in English and tried to shape the living language of Bengali. Such a highly qualified interpreter with one foot in India's cultural past and another all eager to build its future was now sought to be replaced with a class of interpreters who were most likely to start afresh 'in tastes, in opinions, in morals and in intellect' which would have its own advantages and disadvantages.

The idea of having a right kind of interpreter, skilled, loyal and trustworthy, for the British had plagued them since Sir Thomas Roe was jointly dispatched to the Mughal court of Emperor Jehangir in 1615 jointly by the Company and King James I. Bernard S. Cohn tells us how Thomas Roe found it difficult to operate in the culturally and linguistically alien place called India and complained to his employers:

> Another terrible inconvenience that I suffer: want of an interpreter. For the Broker's here will not speak but what shall please, yeah they would alter the King's letter because his name was before the Mughals which I would not allow.[47]

It is this great handicap in understanding, gaining entry to the socio-cultural, linguistic, political and economic structures—texts and contexts, so to say—that prompted later day British policy makers like Macaulay to establish a well-entrenched and well-trained interpreters of cultures and policies in India through the introduction of English education. The introduction of English education first in Bengal, and later in other parts of the country with the intention of creating such insiders as two-way cultural interpreters changed the dynamics of translation and its impact on nation-building process in a significant way. Now the translation of texts and ideas that were happening till now in a limited manner acquired a full grown political and cultural dialogue with literary, linguistic and textual complexities arising among the three types of educated class: one which had only background of the traditional Sanskrit and Persian languages, one which now acquired the knowledge of English and one which knew only a modern Indian language.[48] Moreover, it presented a grand leap forward from the experiments at Fort William College, where the British officials were being taught Indian languages. In this sense, there was a fourth type of educated class occupying Indian space: English officials having smattering of knowledge of some

Indian languages. Further, Empire needed a whole lot of subordinate government officials to run the increasing needs of its administrative and political apparatus, hence the process of creating such a class needed to be started. With the official announcement in 1844 that applicants for government employment should possess knowledge of English, this process got impetus.[49]

Translation from Sanskrit and Persian into Indian Languages

Changing Dynamics

However, despite this historic event, any visible change in the language of the literary discourse was not to be seen as far as creative writings in original are concerned. In fact, throughout the nineteenth century, a strong trend of ancient Sanskrit as well as Persian texts like *Hitopdesa, Panchatantra, Tutinameh,* to name a few, getting translated into Bengali, Hindi, Marathi, Urdu etc can be seen. Actually, during the first half of the 19th century and even after the upheaval of 1857, the modern Indian languages still got their source materials from Sanskrit language texts and from the Persian lanaguges especially in Hindi, Urdu, Punjabi, Sindhi and Kashmiri. The trend is an assertion of nativity—somekind of national consciousness to regain the famed past of the glory of India and reflect that in Indian languages. Another reason of this trend is that Indian languages had their sources in the linguistic and literary traditions of Sanskrit and Persian and turned towards them for creative nourishments. However, the choice of themes is now more towards fiction in prose style. Hence, even the Sanskrit texts get translated with their variants and translation of *Sakuntla* (1854) by Vidyasagar, a prose narrative based on Kaildasa's play, is a case in point and anticipates the dawn of the genre of novel, first in Bengal and gradually in other parts of India.

But Vidyasagar's translation of *Sakuntala* further concretized the vague aspirations of the educated class to find an identity for itself under the colonial subjugation. From the point of view of translations acting as agent of change in language, style and intention, Vidyasagar's *Sakuntala* introduces a crucial element, that of translation into the target language, in Bengali, with deliberately lesser use of Sanskrit idiom. Vidyasgar took the movement initiated by Roy further and very soon the debate about the idiom and style to be used in translating texts into Indian languages and finally the writing of original prose in these languages took a centre stage in all Indian languages by the end of the 19th century extending into the 20th century. Ultimately, this debate acquired socio-cultural connotations and as part of the nation-building process, de-Sanskritisation and de-Persianisation of prose in Indian languages gained impetus with the rise of the English-educated class. This is not surprising, if seen in the proper historical perspective. English-educated class ultimately acquired the power and prestige that the Sanskrit and Persian-educated class had enjoyed till the end of the 19th century and they put their weight behind the advocacy for indigenous elements in Indian languages to make them more people-oriented.

As seen in the context of nation-building process in Europe, in general, and in England, in particular, the national consciousness naturally embraces the language for its expression. The movement for communicating the written text to the masses in their own languages was championed in cultural and political arena by the makers of the new India—Vivekananda, Tilak, Gandhi, Narayan Guru, Periyar, Nehru, Azad etc. Vivekanada led from the front and proclaimed:

> In this country owing to all learning being in Sanskrit from the ancient times, there has arisen an immeasurable gulf between the learned and the common folk. All the great personages, from Buddha, down to

> Chaitanya and Ramakrishna, who came for the well-being of the world, taught the common people in the languages of the people themselves.[50]

Vivekananda and other national leaders who followed, by evoking reformers and movements from India's ancient past, placed their model for communication of ideas to the people right alongside the Sanskritic tradition which also advocated its use in translations and communication on the basis of its links with the glorious past of India. Here, it may be in order to refer to the language used, both linguistic and textual, and the messages given by two most important leaders of national movement—Bal Gangadhar Tilak and Mahatma Gandhi—in interpreting one of the most influential and integral of ancient Hindu texts, *Bhagvadgita*. These interpretations of *Gita* in the midst of national struggle for freedom from the colonial rule should be seen as a way to translate the spirit of the ancient text to the masses at large with the purpose to get across their socio-political views to the last reader.

Tilak, in his *Gita-Rahasya*, written in Marathi to get the message across to the common Marathi reader, evoked Krishna's injunction to Arjuna to take up arms and perform his duty as a warrior, to underline his belief in violent struggle to lead the country to freedom. But, Gandhi, in his interpretation of the message of *Gita*, written in his mother-tongue, Gujarati, viewed the teachings of the Gita as an allegorical representation of the conflict between knowledge and ignorance, within each person, and insisted upon the centrality of the Gita's teaching that we must perform our duties without expecting the fruits of our labour—underlining his non-violent approach to national struggle for freedom. However, as interpreters, they emphasize and succeed in getting across their political belief as well as the need to be genuine interpreters of ancient wisdom for the common people in the language of the common people without being pedantic.

In this context, it is interesting to quote what a biographer of Sree Narayan Guru states while talking about interpretation of *Gita* and other *Upanishadic* philosophy by the Guru for the understanding of the common people of Kerala of his time:

> They have a distressing brevity, presenting as they do, the distilled essence of the *Upanishadic* philosophy with startling suggestions and novel interpretations...Excellent in dignified statement and depth of thought as they are we are struck by his use of small, ordinary, old Malayalam words which have been lost in the market-place of daily usage.[51]

However, the trend of, what may be viewed as *Prakritisation*[52] which is seen throughout the 19th and 20th century nation-building process in Bangla, Marathi, Tamil, Kannada, Malayalam, Gujarati, Oriya, Hindi, Urdu, Punjabi etc and acquired new meanings in different contexts with some linguistic groups going overboard and making it their central concern of identity. In Tamil, translation process acquired a deeply political connotation with Sanskrit being seen not only as the language of the elites but also representative of the North Indian/Aryan hegemony. In Malayalam, both Sanskrit and Tamil were viewed as alien and efforts were made to project the indigenous Malayalam elements in the modern language. The de-Persianisation and de-Sanskritisation approach acquired monstrous proportions in the North with cultural and religious identities shaping the literary and linguistic discourse in terms of Hindi-Urdu controversy ultimately playing a vital role in the partition of India; and in the South leading to calls for separatism as a reaction against the Brahaminical social structures and hegemony of Sanskrit on Dravidian languages, especially Tamil. However, the movements for

'Pure Malayalam' or *pucca Malayalam*, or for that matter the 'Pure Tamil' or *Tanil-Tamil Iyakkam* realized the limitations of obliterating linguistic borrowings in totality as something impractical as well as undesirable.

Translation of Ideas, Literary Models and Texts from English Language to Indian Languages: Tension between Form and Content

However, for a proper understanding of this movement towards the indigenous languages and making them a vehicle of socio-cultural identity, the 'role' and contribution of the translation from English texts to these languages need to be understood. The intervention of the English texts into Indian language translation, literary as well as those related to other fields of enquiry, like the sciences, archeology, philosophy, history, biographies and autobiographies etc. introduces the best as well as the worst in European cultural discourse and are led or modulated by that 'class of interpreters' which Macaulay wanted to create. On the level of ideas and scientific enquiry, these English texts opened up new windows to the world and despite cultural and religious reforms initiated by leaders like Dayanand Saraswati, for example, along with the texts, the notion of the cultural superiority of the West also got translated and communicated to the Indian language audience. Hence there was a continuous, and continued, tension between what text to take for translation and how to reflect that in Indian languages, and also how to Indianise Western literary models for successful use here.

A case in point is the translation of Shakespeare. Following the translation of Bible into various Indian languages at the turn of the 19th century, some of the texts that got translated from English into various Indian languages included texts like *The Pilgrim's Progress,*

Gulliver's Travels, Aesop's Fables, Robinson Crusoe etc. However, after 1850, some attempts to translate Shakespeare started with the first Bengali translation of the play, *The Merchant of Venice,* appearing in 1853 under the title *Bhanumati Cittavilas* by Haran Chandra Ghosh.[53] The process got a fillip in the last decades of the 19th century and at the turn of 20th century with many of Shakesperean plays getting translated or adapted for the stage performances as well as classroom teaching. But this needs to be understood that teaching of Shakespeare and translation of his plays into Indian languages took place under the entrenched parameters of the colonial-colonised framework in India after the introduction of English education system. What it did in terms of shaping the Indian sensibility and taste is summarized very effectively by Sisir Kumar Das:

> Shakespeare was translated into French and Moliere into English by competent bilinguals, the reputation of Shakespeare in France or Moliere in England respectively rested almost entirely on these translations, and not on the opinion of a handful of scholars who could read them in the original. In India, on the contrary, Shakespeare translations began when English education was more or less firmly established and a sizeable population of English-knowing people had emerged, and Shakespeare had become a cultural icon for the elite.[54]

This notion of Shakespeare being the greatest playwright belonging to the Empire motivated translations of his plays into Indian languages and those who took up translations into languages also sought to use the content and forms of his plays for making socio-cultural statements. In the preface to his *Vikara-Vilasita* (1883), the Marathi translation of *Hamlet,* the eminent social reformer Gopal Ganesh Agarkar (1856–1895) and a close associate of Tilak, who worked a lot for Marathi language, stated that one of the major objectives of reading the plays of other cultures is to realize the limitations of one's own society:

> Those who advocate child-marriage, or the tonsuring of the heads of the young widows, or are engaged in debates on the appropriate size of one's turban or codes of dress during meals, or whether the husband should address his wife by her name and feel proud of such things need not read *Othello* or *Lear* or *Romeo and Juliet.*[55]

Coming from an eminent social reformer, who fell out with Tilak on the issue of emphasizing more on social reforms in the Indian society than on its political freedom, the observation above shows a sentiment coming from a translator who interprets the Shakespearean drama as a way to express the sentiments of the marginal classes in Indian society. Another point of tension is the ambivalence of the translators towards the model that Shakespearean plays presented as opposed to the existing ancient model of Sanskrit theatre. There were translators who opened up to Shakespeare but also kept translating Kalidasa's plays to show their continued interest in the native classical models. Talking about the Kannada scene in the last decades of 19th century, R S Mugali states:

> Basavappa Sastri known as *Abhinava Kalidasa*, produced fine renderings of *Abhijana Sakuntala, Uttararamacharita* and *Chandakrusika.* His translation of Shakespeare's *Othello* under the title *Sura Sena Carita* was the fine example of foreign influence in creative writing known to us. It was published in 1895.[56]

Some of the other authors from English who were frequently translated into Indian languages included Milton, Dryden, Shelley, Wordsworth, Tennyson and, later in the 20th century, W. B Yeats and T.S Eliot.

However, in the framework of colonial-colonized relationship, it is not only the texts, but the literary canons or models also get transplanted from the ruler to the ruled and play far more reaching and penetrative role. K. Satchidanand puts it in proper perspective:

> The British however had sought to bulldoze and standardize India`s diverse literary culture through a strictly policed translation activity done "under close Western supervision`` by the English or anglicised Indians, following Western tastes, norms and sensibilities. They also encouraged and awarded Indian language writing of "approved design and style.`` Susie Tharu in her essay "The Arrangement of an Alliance`` has cited several examples to prove that a remarkable number of novels in the Indian languages were responses to "an ideological ambience in which a totally new sense of responsibilities of the writer as well as the social function of literature and literary study featured prominently.`` A new idea of the aesthetic was in the making, along with a new politics and a new economy that demanded a faithful adherence to its own norms and proportions.[57]

The case of Micheal Madhusudan Dutt's (1824–1873) epic in Bengali, *Meghanad Badh Kavya*, which he wrote after re-discovering his 'mother-tongue' after years of uncritical Westernized outlook and lifestyle, is quite integral to this concept of transplanting western literary models into Indian languages under immediate colonial impact. Dutt made his intention very clear when he wrote:

> It is my ambition to engulf the exquisite graces of the Greek mythology on our own…You shan't have to complain against the un-Hindu character of the poem…I shall not borrow Greek stories but write, rather try to write as Greeks would have done.[58]

It is this fascination for the western literary traditions and models that also inspired the writing of novels in India. The genre of novel, popularized by Bankim Chand Chatterjee, who incidentally wrote his first novel in English titled *Rajmohan' Wife,* and followed by other pioneering novelists like Hari Naryan Apte, Chandu Menon, Fakir Mohan Senapati, Rabindranath Tagore, Rajnikanta Bordoloi, Bhai Vir Singh, Sarat Chandra Chattopadhyay, Premchand etc. was certainly fashioned after the Victorian genre of novel made popular by the writers like Charles Dickens and George Eliot. Initially, most of the novelists took their inspiration from the historical novels of Sir Walter Scott weaving romances related to land and the people, before finding their own voice by turning to social realism and political novels. However, despite the Western model, the novelists in Indian languages could recognize, interpret and express the growing sense of nationalism especially after the advent of Mahatma Gandhi on the scene. As Gandhi's image got towering and while constantly being a foil to the meta-narrative of the Colonial rule, he himself was canonized and portrayed as hero, many a time symbolically, in various fictional works as in Premchand. In the 20th century, the impact of T S Eliot on the 'modern' poetry in different Indian languages, is something that goes beyond the imitation of literary models. In many cases even the emotional vacuity and the sense of boredom and cynicism that his poetry expressed in the aftermath of the First World War were all sought to be transplanted by the poets in India. Sisir Kumar Das quotes the historian of Oriya literature, Mansingh, who viewed

> with sarcasm how the progressives made the 'poor rickshawallah' the most glamorous hero, unknown to himself and how suddenly he went back to oblivion and the 'field is now crowded with pseudo little Ezra Pounds and pseudo little Eliots.'[59]

The genre of literary criticism too got fashioned after the modern English/Western critical tradition.

However, it is interesting to underline that not only the serious fiction or poetry tried to fit in and imported its forms and models from the West, the genre of popular literature, for example, detective novels and thrillers also got their inspiration from Arthur Conan Doyle, Wilkie Collins etc. In Tamil, for example, the sleuth Govindan of the novelist J R Rangaraju (1875–1956) 'was the Tamil incarnation of Sherlock Holmes.'[60] The same is true of other areas of discipline in their attempts to construct them following the rise of nationalism. Writing about the experiments done by Maharaja Ayilyam Tirunal of Travancore (1861–75) to publish books for the Malayali reader of his state under the Text Book Committee with the eminent poet and scholar Kerala Verma as the Chairperson, P. K Parameswaran Nair writes:

> The publication which Kerala Verma brought out were primers for the first three standards, text books on the histories of Travancore and India, one on geography, another on economics and a book of essays called *Vijnanamanjari*...The only guides he had in their writing were similar text books in English...[61]

Actually, in the grand Colonial design of introducing English education into India during the 19th century, the Indian response was not based on scientific and historical parameters. Even those who opposed it could not present any alternative before the masters. As Bipan Chandra puts it so very matter-of-factly:

> Unfortunately, there was a great deal of confusion on this question. Many people failed to distinguish between English as a medium and English as a subject for study and between Indian languages as a medium and traditional Indian learning as the main object of study.[62]

As we find throughout the nineteenth century, even the most learned men advocated English education in the name of modern and scientific knowledge thereby creating a schism between what was desired and what was being communicated. One may say that perhaps a clearheaded interpreter of the changing times like Raja Ram Mohun Roy would have been able to translate it all for his audience and for the colonial masters had he been placed in the later half of the 19th century.

Translation among Indian Languages and Inter-Relationship with Indian English: Emergence of New Hierarchies and Dialectics

Edward P. Rice, whose *A History of Kannada Literature* was first published in 1921, made a factual observation of translation works being done in Kannada at that time which proves to be an interesting pointer to the trends prevailing at that time:

> Novels are becoming increasingly popular. Most of those hitherto published have been reproductions from English or Bengali. Several of the plays of Shakespeare have been reproduced in this form, e.g; *Bharat Vilasa* (Comedy of Errors); also such works as Sir Conan Doyle's detective stories of Sir Sherlock Holmes. The Bengali works of Bankim Chandra Chattopadhyay and of Surendra Nath have been reproduced, chiefly by Mr. B. Venkatacharya, a retired munsif. The most esteemed of these are the *Durgeshanandini* and *Devichandhurani.*[63]

In the above para, the new element that we encounter for the first time is reference to the translation of Bangla books into Kannada. This is a trend that will play its integrative role in nation-building, the next step for the Indian educated class to discover more about their own land and languages and culture, but at the same time this will also underline the new fusion of power and culture in the changing Indian scenario. The early lead taken by Bengal because of it being the site of colonial experiments is reflected in the books from Bengali getting translated into other Indian languages including Oriya, Hindi, Marathi, Kannada etc with the novels of Bankimchand Chatterjee and later the works of Tagore being the most popular texts for translation. This interaction between Indian languages is a major change and a vehicle of discovery of different cultures and customs prevalent in various parts of the country. In fact, the case of Kannada is typical as B. Venkatacharya translated almost the entire works of Bankim Chanda into Kannada with many believing that they are his own.[64] Translation from Marathi and Hindi into other languages also picked up in the 20th century.

Another element that came into play in the 20th century is the complete institutionalization of the English language as the language of the powerful, not only because of its legacy, but also because of it being the language of inter-cultural dialogue, both in the Indian context and in international scenario. The success that embraced Tagore in the form of his becoming the first Asian to receive Nobel Prize for Literature in 1913 following the publication of the English translation of his work *Gitanjali* started a new trend. It not only recognized the importance of Indian works getting translated into English for national and global recognition, but also gave a fillip to translation among Indian languages with English acting as the mediator. The trend of English texts getting translated into Indian languages and those of Indian languages into English can not, however, be seen only in the sense of English language gaining and retaining a pivotal position in the socio-cultural and literary discourse of India. The counter-narrative coming in the form of enquiries 'below', from the women, dalit, tribal communities, utilize the power of English language to position their perspectives on the national and international mainstream platform, rather many a time they alter the agenda of the discourse. It should be seen as the achievement of nationalism and post-colonialism that English language, whether the texts get translated on linguistic plane or on ideological plane, itself has undergone changes with Indianness defining its grammar, its vocabulary, and its idiom in a significant manner as far as discourses from India and about India is concerned.

In this context, the comment of Renate Zahar about the ambivalent attitude to the language of the colonizer by the colonized is instructive:

> As a rule, it can be said that the relation of the colonized toward the language of the colonial dominator is ambivalent. He covets and respects it as a means of social climbing, while at the same time hating and dreading it as an instrument of colonial rule.[65]

In fact, as an ultimate triumph of nationalism, we find that though many national leaders, Jawaharlal Nehru, for example, mostly used English for written as well as oral communication, the socio-cultural and political language that they used carried decidedly national and anti-imperial messages. Nehru's *Discovery of India* as well as his historic 'Tryst with Destiny' speech are communicated in English and on textual plane no translation as such happens, but we know for sure that Nehru is interpreting the long history and heritage of India for the contemporary generation and trying to translate for them what it means to stand in the backdrop of and in the context of an India emerging as a nation-state from the wombs of India as a colony.

Having said this, the new hierarchy that Indian-English has created links it up with the linguistic scenario of the 18th and 19th century, when Persian and, to some extent, Sanskrit languages were symbols of power and of literary discourse. The recognition and success that have lately come to Indian English writers in the international arena have led to the debate between literature written in Indian languages and those in Indian English as to which is more representative of Indian scenario. Considering the vast linguistic and social and cultural upheaval through which India as a nation-state has emerged from the concept of India as a civilization, it is likely that the debate will ultimately be settled on the basis of the social, cultural and political language of the works rather than on its philological language thus requiring translators to be more evolved and empathetic interpreters. In this context, the continuous interpretative nature of modern Indian writers and translators, placed as they are in the aftermath of the colonial experience, is aptly put by Nirmal Verma, the noted Hindi writer, when he quotes a contemporary Indian philosopher, J. L. Mehta, and can be used to sign off this continuing discussion in the present context:

> There is no other way open to us in the East, but to go along with Europeanization and to go through it. Only through this voyage into the foreign and strange can we win back our own selfhood; hence, here as elsewhere, the way to do what is closest to us is the longest way back.[66]

'Nation Building and the Dynamics of Translation' was written for the MA Translation Unit book of Indira Gandhi National Open University, New Delhi and was published by the University in Hindi translation as a Booklet.

CHAPTER 10

POST-COLONIALISM AND BEYOND

Reading Edward W. Said in the Context of Contemporary Dalit Literary Discourse in India

Post-Colonialism as an 'ism' offers interesting contradictions even though it stems from the overall commitment to the 'representation of reality' from the perspective of the subaltern or the 'Other', a term which acquires different robes in different contexts. In the context of global discourse, it is the previously colonized nations of the Third World, which are the subaltern or the Other vis-a vis the traditional colonial powers of the First World; in the context of races, it is Black vs. the White; in the Gender discourse, it is Women vs. Men (the recent discussion about 'western' vs. 'non-western feminism' has now added a new dimension) and in the purely Indian context it is the Dalits and religious minorities which represent the term in relation to the Upper Castes of the Hindu society. The discourse between the 'Overseas East' and 'Metropolitan West' with all their connotations is another manifestation of the umbrella topic of the post-colonial examination. Michel Foucault put it rather succinctly when he stated, "Post-Colonialism is a complicated theory with many meanings."

These are just some of the contexts in which post-colonial postures become valid from the stand point of the hitherto unacknowledged, unrepresented or misrepresented 'Other' because the inherent contradictions in human societies across all spaces and all times can not allow a fixed definition of the colonial and the colonized, oppressor and the oppressed. A community identified with the oppressors in one context becomes the oppressed in some other. Hence, in simpler terms, one may say that post-colonialism re-examines the relationship between the oppressor and the oppressed from the perspective of the latter and this re-examination or 'counter-narrative' opens up new vistas of discourse which can always be given, to borrow a phrase from Shakespeare, 'a local name and habitation' to understand their relevance in our immediate context.

Against this backdrop, the relevance of Edward W Said (1935–2003), arguably one of the most accomplished and visionary post-colonial theorists in our times, assumes significance. Here we are not talking about his seminal work, *Orientalism*, but actually looking at the large number of his essays on the contemporary literary and cultural issues[1] which tirelessly and successfully, to an extent, took post-colonial discourse beyond the narrow confines of, what he said 'reverse racism' or nationalism. Born on 1st November, 1935 in Palestine, from where his family got settled in Egypt after getting exiled from there following the creation of Israel in 1948, Said transformed his personal traumatic experience of imperialism into the understanding of imperial excesses and hypocrisy as a world wide phenomenon through his scholarship. However, it was to his credit that he did not allow his personal experiences of receiving continued death threats and hostilities in America (where he taught Comparative Literature for almost four decades at Columbia University) for supporting the cause of his native Palestinians to come in the way of recognizing the need to understand imperialism and post-imperialism in its entirety, wherein the issue was not to substitute the Euro-centric view of the world with an Africa-centric or Asia-centric one, but to point out the 'politics of knowledge' played by the colonial powers in order to overcome it. Instead of giving 'implicit concessions to European ethnocentrism and supremacist thought'[2], he advocated, 'the amalgamation between Europe and its imperium acting together in the process of decolonization.'

Thus, the issues Said raises and discusses acquires pointed relevance in the context of contemporary Dalit literary discourse in the country, which, rightfully, has emerged as a significant post-colonial tool to re-examine hitherto 'established' modes of expressing the position of man/woman in the Indian society and re-defines the relationship between the dominant and the subaltern. A reading of Said mainly on the counts of the claims of 'exclusivity' of Dalit literature, its response to the literature of the 'colonial era' and its relationship with the contemporary 'mainstream' literature may take the Dalit discourse further.

A major point of discussion in the Dalit discourse revolves around the contention that only a Dalit can portray the sense of discrimination, humiliation and stigma attached to the life of a Dalit in the Indian society. A non-Dalit writing and talking about the Dalit issues can, despite best of his intentions and commitment, only have a sympathetic ring to his approach as he does not possess the personal experience required to express the innermost feelings of a Dalit. On the face of it, the argument sounds convincing, however, a Said reader is exposed to the other side of this argument, which makes him take a fresh look at it. For Said, such an approach is defeatist and actually reactionary. In the Introduction to his collection of essays *Reflections on Exile and Other Cultural and Literary Essays*, he states:

> The historical experience of imperialism for the imperialized entailed subservience and exclusion; therefore the historical experience of national resistance and decolonization was designed for liberation and inclusion.[3]

Further, he adds,

> When such notions of insider privilege are advanced they have to be rejected out of hand as perpetuations of the exclusions one should always oppose, a sort of racism or nationalism by imitation, which in this book I have criticized both in supposedly privileged or "objective" observers like Naipaul and Orwell, both of them renowned for the transparency and "honesty" of their style, and in social insiders like Walter Lippmann. Like all style, "good" or transparent writing has to be demystified with the power that allows it to *be there* ...[4]

When Said points out that such expressions of exclucism was 'the direct result of either forgetting or rejecting this edifying equation' resulting in a degenerative nationalism, its parallel in the Dalit discourse appears quite striking. Dalit writing as the exclusive domain of the Dalits is actually a later–day phenomenon and was not designed that way by the pioneering first generation of Dalit writers. One of the resolutions adopted at the first conference of Dalit writers organized in Bombay by the Maharashtra Dalit Sahitya Sangha in 1958 which originally coined the term 'Dalit Literature' reads thus:

> Resolution No. 5—that the literature written by the Dalits and that written by others about the Dalits in Marathi be accepted as a

> separate entity known as "Dalit Literature" and realizing its cultural importance, the universities and literary organizations should give it proper place.[5]

In this context, Said refers to the eminent Nigerian writer Wole Soyinka who attacked brilliantly Senghor's *negritude* in the 1960s 'for its defeatism', but thirty years later attacked 'the well known Kenyan political theorist Ali Mazuri for not being enough of a "pure" African'. Said here quite subtly reveals the fine thread that separates a reactionary from the progressive, the oppressor from the oppressed and how changing milieu demands continued sifting of reality in order to shun the privileges which any kind of power necessarily bestows in a particular context.

This brings us to the issue of the post-colonial/Dalit response to the literature produced from the point of view of the western/ Brahamanical observer at the centre of the consciousness in the global/Indian context. From the standpoint of his own approach and by referring to the works of post-colonial writers like Aime Cesaire, Fanon, W.E.B Du Bois, Toni Morrison, etc. Said points out that the pioneering liberationist movement though believed that

> racial thought and the persecution of the black individual were the responsibility of aspects of white or European mainstream culture, but they did not mean that *all* whites and Europeans, or *all* white and European culture, were to be thrown out and rejected.[6]

Said makes a special mention of the integrative approach of Toni Morrison, the celebrated 'black' Nobel Laureate who in her book *Playing in the Dark: Whiteness and the Literary Imagination* instead of taking the simpler route of making 'sentimental appeal to…nativist genre', she 'discusses… instances of the master narrative, works by Poe, Mark Twain, Hemingway, Cather, whose significance on aesthetic and historical grounds is granted in a manner that is neither hectoring nor vengeful.'[7] By taking an integrative approach Morrison becomes a part of the historical process of debate on how literature heightens our understanding of our immediate life.

If we compare this to the general trend in Dalit literary response to the literature of the 'high caste', the integrative approach is yet to take roots. Even a senior and respectful Dalit writer like Baburao Bagul, who, in an essay promisingly titled 'Dalit Literature is But Human Literature' fails to broaden the definition of 'Human' beyond the term 'Dalit'. The last paragraph of the essay reads thus:

> The established literature of India is Hindu literature. But it is Dalit literature which has the revolutionary power to accept new science and technology and bring about a total transformation. 'Dalit' is the name for total revolution; it is revolution incarnate.[8]

This attitude of absolute rejection is most recently seen in Hindi Dalit literary discourse too. A look at the contents of the Special Issue on Dalit Discourse brought out by the leading literary magazine *Hans* edited by the eminent litterateur Rajendra Yadav bears this out. In this 242 page issue interspersed with contemporary Dalit poetry, short stories, criticism and interviews, one would find that there is not a single write-up dedicated to the textual re-examination of any 'established' author or work of the Hindi literature of the past in the light of the Dalit discourse. This is all the more surprising because the issue has been brought out on the occasion of 125th birth anniversary of Premchand, now under the scan of Dalit criticism (and incidentally the founder of the said magazine). In fact, Yadav's editorial could bring himself to write about Premchand only as a representative of an 'elite class, who was reviewed and declared timeless by people of this very class'.[9]

In the light of Said's observation that Toni Morrison *et al* give 'very persuasive and eloquent arguments ... for *including* and *remembering* (Said's italics), rather than for merely giving focus to or encoding crucial historical experiences', one feels that some more debate is required in the Dalit discourse on how to respond to the masterpieces of the past. Said himself examines his own approach which needs serious consideration on the part of the present day 'post-colonial critic' in the country. He states:

> Far from rejecting or disqualifying canonical writers because of crudely political considerations, my approach has tried to re-situate writers in their own history with a particular emphasis on those apparently marginal aspects of their work which because of the historical experience of non- European readers have acquired a new prominence.[10]

This approach is most evident in Said's examination of Joseph Conrad who, as Said finds, in a novel like *Heart of Darkness* can see through the hypocritical and corrupting influence of Western imperialism as prevailing in Africa, but the particular period of history that he inhabited did not allow him to see beyond that to have a vision of the corrupt imperialism from the perspective of the imperialized.

Edward Said consistently argues for enlarging the scope of the post-colonial discourse. This is in keeping with the approach of the confirmed anti-imperial writers like Fanon, Cesaire etc. The fact that there is only one 'worldly cultural space, the common possession of all humankind, and also a universal language of rights and ideals in which to wage the struggle for liberation and inclusion' need not be lost sight of. When we talk of historical experience, we are also acknowledging the historical space shared by both the colonial and the colonized and no discourse can take place in isolation to each other. As Said puts it so eloquently:

> ...what distinguished the great liberationist cultural movements that stood against Western imperialism was that they wanted liberation within the same universe of discourse inhabited by Western culture. As Cesaire put it in his greatest poem (in a phrase echoed and re-echoed by C L R James), "no race has a monopoly on beauty, or intelligence, or strength, and there is room for everyone at the convocation of conquest."[11]

Actually, it is not only C L R James, but Said himself quotes these words of Cesaire again and again to drive home the point that post-colonial discourse should be able to get beyond the idea of writing back to the empire as that limits its historically progressive note that it is expected to carry on.

That there can be a separate non-Western/Dalit discourse away from the 'mainstream' discourse is a vision neither feasible nor welcome. The 'Other' needs to enter into a dialogue about the concepts of justice, beauty, aesthetics etc on an equal footing with the dominant to influence, to make its presence felt in the only available secular cultural space occupied by all mortals. And this engagement with the dominant needs more than only 'counter-narrative' or testimonies of suppression. As someone who vouched for the Palestinians as the epitome of victimhood and who was branded by many Western critics as a militant intellectual, the larger view that Said offers shows his high scholarship and commitment for literature as well as humanity. He states:

> Victimhood, alas, does not guarantee or necessarily enable an enhanced sense of humanity. To testify to a history of oppression is necessary, but it is not sufficient unless that history is redirected into intellectual process and universalized to include all sufferers.[12]

This is actually the crux of Saidian philosophy and demands a more mature response from Dalit thinkers. When the critic Sisir

Kumar Das in the multi-volume compilation of Indian Literature undertaken by Sahitya Akademi referred to Dalit Literature as a 'narrative of suffering' it was justifiably objected to by Dalit critics as a manifestation of condescending attitude of the 'elites' to the Dalit Literature. However, when Gail Omvedt states,

> "And since they (the Dalits) are more human, more interesting and dramatic and have a more truthful cause than their Brahamanical and upper caste opponents, they are winning a market as well",[13]

one's reading of Said's views on victimhood vis-a-vis humanity makes one ponder over the issue once again.

Some discussions on these lines have taken place among Dalit thinkers also. That literature to become more enduring needs more than the expression of anger and humiliation is pointed out by R G Jadhav in his essay "Dalit Feelings and Aesthetic Detachment', wherein he states:

> ....social consciousness in Dalit poetry is getting standardized. This poetry is becoming confined to provocative emotional outbursts. It is getting set into the usual moulds of revolt, helplessness and protest. In a way this is natural. But it has lent the music of repetitive social notes to Dalit poetry....Though Dalit feelings are broadly the same, they require distinction in their individual existence.[14]

The 'distinction in individual existence' that Jadhav talks about is actually not only a problem of aesthetic detachment; it is also the outcome of the unwillingness to redirect the testimony of personal historical suffering to 'universalize' it to include all sufferers, because as stated at the outset, there can not be a fixed notion of oppressor as well as oppressed. In fact, the basic premise of post-colonialism, when it rejects the notion of 'master-narrative' of the West, is that it believes in 'multiple centres' and looks at the experiences and backgrounds of different groups as well as discourses, which, in turn, can offer multiple-narratives. And it is the response to this question of universalizing the pain of suffering among the Dalit community and beyond it, of offering multiple-narratives that will determine the future direction of Dalit literary discourse. This high expectation from Dalit discourse is also indicative of the significant historical position that it takes in the list of discourses in the country through the ages.

It is a slightly revised version of the paper written in 2005 and later published on Academia.edu platform in 2014.

CHAPTER 11

THE CHANGING DYNAMICS OF NEGRITUDE MOVEMENT AND PAN-AFRICAN IDENTITY

Reading the Poem "Prayer to Masks" by Léopold Sédar Senghor

Léopold Sédar Senghor (1906–2001) was the legendary Senegalese poet, politician, and cultural theorist who for two decades served as the first president of Senegal (1960–1980), a country in West Africa, previously a French colony before attaining independence in 1960. He is credited, with Martiniqan poet and theorist Aimé Césaire (1913–2008), and the Guianan Léon Damas (1912–1978)—the 'Three Fathers', as popularly referred to— to have founded the *negritude movement* in the 1930s as a kind of a common black identity to counter and reject the French colonial racism. Senghor, as a negritude writer, searched for the intrinsic reality and splendour of the Black experience and portrayed African life with dignity and almost with a sense of ecstasy.

Advocating a Pan-African identity, as opposed to the white/ Europe-centric one, Senghor argued that 'far from seeing in one's blackness inferiority, one accepts it; one lays claim to it with pride; one cultivates it lovingly'. Senghor's negritude received a kind of an endorsement by the most influential of modern French thinkers and statesmen, Jean Paul-Sartre (1905–1980), who termed it as an "antiracist racism", stating in the Preface to Senghor's 1948 anthology titled *Poems of a Black Orpheus* representing Francophone poetry:

> A Jew, a white among whites, can deny that he is a Jew, declaring himself a man among men. The black cannot deny that he is black nor claim for himself an abstract, colorless humanity: he is black. Thus he is driven to authenticity: insulted, enslaved, he raises himself up. He picks up the word "black" ["N*gre"] that they had thrown at him like a stone, he asserts his blackness, facing the white man, with pride.[1]

However, the negritude movement seemed to be riding on a double-edged theory—emphasising the colour of skin to reclaim the African identity, and thus, at the same time, dangerously pandering to the white-black racial discrimination and inequality as advocated by the White and canonical supremacists. In fact, Senghor went on to say in one of his many scholarly articles on the idea of negritude that "emotion is black as reason is Greek"—thus sounding perilously very close to the White narrative.

As a result, later, the younger Black poets and theorists like Franz Fanon, Chinua Achebe, Wol Soyinka et al in the 1960s onward had rather complex engagement with negritude—refining it, critiquing it, and bringing out the individuality of self and the complex and plural voices that make up the idealised 'Pan-African' identity. In fact, Wole Soyinka, the poet-playwright-novelist from Nigeria, the first African to receive a Nobel Prize for Literature in 1986, proved to be the severest critic of the Pan-African and negritude ideas of Senghor. Soyinka, who came under criticism from critics associated with the Negritude movement for his use of European literary techniques, cautioned his Negritude critics against promoting a stereotypical dichotomy between Western rationalism and African emotionalism, and considered Negritude as a nostalgic and indiscriminate glorification of the black African past that ignores the potential benefits of modernisation. He famously wrote, "A tiger does not proclaim its tigritude. It pounces."[2]

While, Soyinka's criticism was symptomatic of the complexity involved in developing a homogenous concept of Pan-Africanism, it further got complicated when Soyinka himself found himself at odds with the question of Arab/Islamic contribution to the making of African culture and identity as advocated by the Kenyan-born distinguished socio-political critic and statesman Ali Al'amin Mazrui. The changing dynamics of Pan-African Identity is so very well captured by Edward W. Said in the 'Introduction' to his *Reflections on Exile and Other Literary and Cultural Essays,* who, while talking of the 'great deal of nativism and violently separatist thought in the anti-imperialist nationalism of mid-twentieth century', states:

> 'Thus the celebrated Nigerian writer Wole Soyinka attacks Senghor's negritude in the early 1960s—attacks it brilliantly and resourcefully for its defeatism, its implicit concessions to European ethnocentrism and supremacist thought—and then thirty years later in his own journal *Transition* attacks the well-known Kenyan political theorist Ali Mazrui for not being enough of 'pure' African.'[3]

Actually, Soyinka in the early 1990s, in an essay titled 'Religion and Human Rights' published in *Index to Censorship*[4] (1988), felt that Ali Mazrui's immensely popular BBC's television series, *The Africans: A Triple Heritage*, gave prominence to the Christian and Islamic contribution to the making of African identity, and quite ironically, Soyinka talked of 'African authenticity' and went on to denigrate the Islamic traditions of Africa as something alien and pitched for the production of a new television series on Africa to be made 'from a black African perspective.' Soyinka followed up his criticism with another article titled 'Triple Tropes of Trickery', published in his journal *Transition (1991)*, perhaps to which Edward Said refers to above. Ali Mazrui, famous for his debating skills, stated in his essay *Wole Soyinka as a Television Critic: A Parable of Deception* in 1991,

> I do not need Wole Soyinka's stamp of confirmation that I am an African. My identity is in my blood, my ancestry, my history, my commitment, my life. If I was somebody constantly looking for approval from people who were "blacker" than me, I would have kept a low profile instead of becoming a controversial African political analyst.[5]

He painfully asks, "Why is Soyinka taking us down this fascist path of racial quantification and genetic explanation?"

Suddenly, we find that Ali Mazuri's concerns get aligned with those of Maulana Azad, when he, battling the similar 'racial quantification and genetic explanation' in India famously said,

> I am a Muslim and profoundly conscious of that fact that I have inherited Islam's glorious tradition of the last thirteen hundred years. I am not prepared to lose even a small part of that legacy. The history and teachings of Islam, its art and letters, its culture and civilization are part of my wealth and it is my duty to cherish and guard them... But, with all these feelings, I have another

> equally deep realization born out of my life's experience, which is strengthened and not hindered by the Islamic spirit. I am equally proud of the fact that I am an Indian, an essential part of the indivisible unity of Indian nationhood, a vital factor in its total makeup, without which this noble edifice will remain incomplete. I am an essential element, which has gone to build India. I can never surrender this claim.[6]

This debate in Africa, as in India, keeps recurring and confronting us on daily basis.

In the changing perspectives about African Identity, Senghor's negritude, thus, has also been seen as a kind of Black all-encompassing humanism, a la Walt Whitman's—without denying the revolutionary and historical role of the rise of the idea of negritude. This needs to be underlined that Senghor, as the first President of the independent Senegal for twenty years from 1960, realised the whole lot of repression and violence emanating from various African countries reeling under dictatorship and inter-ethnic strifes, and sought greater engagement with the West, which helped provide stability to the newly independent nation.

Let us then read, his beautiful and powerful poem "Prayer to Masks" (Prière aux masques), published in 1945 in his poetry collection *Songs of Darkness* (*Chants d'Ombre*).[7] The poem, besides being a commentary on the historical relationship of dominant/ suppressed between Europe and Africa, brings out a black man's longing for a spiritual and emotional state of being which the enforced inferiority and bestial repression of the colonial/white/western world has snatched from him and his contemporaries. However, in the light of the changing dynamics of debate about what constitutes African identity, here the symbol of 'masks' seems to acquire meanings which Senghor perhaps never intended:

"Prayer to Masks"

by Senghor, 1945

Masks! Oh Masks!
Black mask, red mask, you black and white masks,
Rectangular masks through whom the spirit breathes,
I greet you in silence!
And you too, my panterheaded ancestor.
You guard this place, that is closed to any feminine laughter, to any mortal smile.
You purify the air of eternity, here where I breathe the air of my fathers.
Masks of maskless faces, free from dimples and wrinkles.
You have composed this image, this my face that bends
over the altar of white paper.
In the name of your image, listen to me!
Now while the Africa of despotism is dying – it is the agony of a pitiable princess,
Just like Europe to whom she is connected through the naval.
Now turn your immobile eyes towards your children who have been called
And who sacrifice their lives like the poor man his last garment
So that hereafter we may cry 'here' at the rebirth of the world being the leaven that the white flour needs.
For who else would teach rhythm to the world that has
died of machines and cannons?
For who else should ejaculate the cry of joy, that arouses the dead and the wise in a new dawn?
Say, who else could return the memory of life to men with a torn hope?
They call us cotton heads, and coffee men, and oily men.
They call us men of death.
But we are the men of the dance whose feet only gain
power when they beat the hard soil.

English translation of the Poem courtesy: ***http://allpoetry.com***

CHAPTER 12

BABA NAGARJUN

The Outsider as a 'Peoples' Poet'

One of the earliest poems of the Hindi-Maithili poet Nagarjun (1911–1998) titled 'Unko Pranam', which can be translated as 'Obeisance to Them' published in 1936 when the poet was 25 years old, shows him as a poet having a post-colonial and inclusive spirit much before these terms became a part and parcel of contemporary social, cultural and literary discourse in India. It is not an all-encompassing romantic inclusiveness speaking for all, but carries very much an acute awareness of the contours of the political and cultural dialogue between the dominant and the dominated, between the colonial and the colonized. The poem is a very conscious attempt at underlining the politics of representation as well as misrepresentation of the historically marginal voices through various poetic imageries. The first two paras run thus:

The work that remained incomplete
I pay my obeisance to them.

Those whose dedicated arrows
Proved either blunted or went astray;
The brave who emptied their quiver
Much before the battle came to the end

— Obeisance to them!
The ones who tried to cross the oceans
In their little boats;
And themselves got submerged therein
Their wishes remaining unarticulated for ever

— Obeisance to them!
(my translation)

A tension between the idiom of the poem, which uses chaste Hindi diction, almost Sanskritised one with a conventional rhyme scheme, and its intention to bring to the fore the 'unparalleled services of those/who shunned publicity' is too apparent and revolutionary. What is remarkable is the rare maturity of tone and seriousness that the poem exudes for a poet in his twenties. It appears that the troubled childhood spent in abject penury and parental neglect propelled an automatic connection with the suffering masses of his Mithila region, which despite its cultural richness remained steeped in ignorance, superstition, exploitation and inequality. Instances of unrecognized, unappreciated, unarticulated aspirations are more a rule than exception but to be able to express them in an effective poem at the height of the euphoria and expectations of the national movement puts Nagarjun at the highest pedestal of subaltern enquiry.

The year 1936 is considered very important in Indian literary history. It is the year in which the Progressive Writers' Association was formed by the left-oriented intellectuals. At its first Conference held at Lucknow with the pioneering Hindi-Urdu novelist Premchand (1880–1936) as its President, the 'manifesto' of the new literature was unfurled. The following aspect of Premchand's presidential address has been quoted often to underline the historical and literary churning that it triggered in Indian literature:

> The literature which does not arouse in us a critical spirit, or satisfies our spiritual needs, which is not 'force-giving' and dynamic, which does not awaken our sense of beauty, which does not make us face the grim realities of life in a spirit of determination, has no use for us today. It cannot even be termed as literature.[1]

It is instructive to find that the intention of Premchand's espousal of the new kind of literature is not very different from the Chilean poet Pablo Neruda's (1904–1973) 'Towards an Impure Poetry', written in 1935 as a prologue to *Green Horse for Poetry* that he edited in Spain before the Civil War broke out there in 1936. The following words have been quoted all across the globe over the years to underline Neruda's response and disdain for old-fashioned romanticism in literature and life which has been seen as a manifesto for a poetry that is socially, culturally and politically alive:

> Let that be the poetry we search for: worn with the hand's obligations, as by acids, steeped in sweat and in smoke, smelling of the lilies and urine, spattered diversely by the trades that we live by, inside the law or beyond it.[2]

Against this historical backdrop, the poetic achievement of Nagarjun, born Vaidyanath Mishra at Darbhanga in Bihar and who acquired the name 'Nagarjun' after the famous Buddhist scholar on embracing Buddhism early in life to study Buddhist literature, is something that can only evoke awe and inspiration among the contemporary generation. It is so because Nagarjun at his own level was already experimenting with both the content and the form of his poetic expressions in a manner that these manifestoes tried to push forth in the form of a well-articulated theory. Moreover, even though, Nagarjun associated himself with the left-oriented and progressive movement in literature, he remained completely individualistic in his approach thereby saving his poetry from getting typecast.

In this respect, he can be compared to D H Lawrence (1885 –1930) who despite getting influenced by the prevailing psycho-analytical theories of the first few decades of the 20th century in the West, proved to be much greater artist than a Virginia Wolf or a James Joyce as he mastered the ideas like the use of stream-of-consciousness technique of storytelling by transcending it altogether. Lawrence was too much conscious—which he euphemistically called 'blood-consciousness'—about the role of society in the making of an individual's psychology. He approached the psychological dilemmas of his characters in the backdrop of their social realities thus never completely fitting in and breathing the high Modernist air of his contemporaries.

In the reverse fashion, Nagarjun, while remaining politically and socially committed, also gave equal emphasis on the uniqueness of each individual which makes his poetry complex and genuine. In his poem *Pachhadh Diya Mere Aastik Ne* (Faith Got the Better of Me), Nagarjun explicitly paints the picture of a momentary surrender to his, what may be termed as, religious conditioning, when, while taking a morning walk, he couldn't help admiring and worshipping the rising sun with 'holy' water and chants of mantras.

For a self- confessed atheist with a Marxist ideology that he was, such an event may not be publicly palatable. However, Nagarjun would rather own it up as something that shows a continuous dialogue between his doubt and faith thus making him a psychologically complex but convincing individual. In an apparently self mocking tone which actually mocks at those individuals and intellectuals who have somehow found finality in their convictions, the poet requests his 'post-graduate' companion to ignore this 'deviation' on his part with the poem ending with these lines:

If ever I refuse to admit…
When did I bow my head?
When did I offer water to the sun?
Then you, Rataneshwar, just quietly smile at my deception…

(my translation)

The poem, which was written in 1964, instantly demands a comparison with his other poem '*Kalpana Ke Putra, Hey Bhagwan*' written almost two decades back in 1946 wherein calling God as a son of human imagination, he states in a belligerent fashion:

Oh! Almighty, the son of imagination
No boon do I desire
Curse me if you can
I long for envy, for suffering
I don't look for peace
Need doubts, confusions and delusions
Restless should I remain day and night
My eyes pouring fire
Remaining perpetually indisciplined
I would never take your name even as an aberration.

(my translation)

Reading the two poems together, one would be on a slippery ground if one thinks that the poet has in any way discarded his rebellious tone. Like the diurnal movement of the earth while remaining fixed on its axis, Nagarjun's poetry moves in a spatial fashion whereby his ideas and emotions go through various phases of churning, guided by an ever inquiring spirit.

In the context of Nagarjun's life, this symbol of spatial movement is all the more apt because while the restlessness of his physical being took him to far off places like Varanasi, Calcutta, Lahore, Delhi, Ceylone, Tibet etc, never allowing him to settle down peacefully, his urge for intellectual enrichment made him a multilingual master of classical Sanskrit, Pali, Prakrit, Hindi, Maithali, Bangla etc. While on the one hand, he acquired deep knowledge of traditional wisdom and philosophy of the ancient India by studying Sanskrit philosophical texts, Buddhist scriptures and manuscripts, he got himself systematically trained into the understanding of Marx and Lenin. At the instance of Rahul Sankrityayan, he plunged himself to the Peasants' Movement in Bihar led by Swami Sahajanand Saraswati landing himself behind the bars many a time. From the Naxalite movement to the socialist movement to the students' movement led by Jayaprakash Narayan, Nagarjun got deeply associated with all the major anti-establishment political movements that seized the imagination of the masses in the country.

However, even though he spoke against the established mores, he never shied away from criticizing any attempt to forge some kind of system or establishment of its own by the anti-establishment activists or intellectuals as his concerns drove sustenance from the poor, the exploited, the wronged, the unsung and the unwept masses. His 12-line poem *Jankavi* (The Peoples' Poet) written in 1947 which has its rather grand and nihilistic climax in the poem titled *Mantra-Kavita* written in 1969, shows the utter disdain with which he viewed such contemporary political movements which slid into mere propoaganda and sloganeering reducing themselves to somekind of dogma. It is this ever-wandering urge, not only physically but also intellectually that made Nagarjun a perpetual dissenter and a non-conformist to the core—an outsider, who was deeply entrenched in social realities, combining levity with seriousness as in *Mantra Kavita*. Not surprisingly, because of this self-mocking and intensely satirical tone that dared to attack hypocrisies of all hues, Hindi critics, Prof. Namwar Singh as well as Vishnu Khare, compared him with Kabir, a comparison which seems more appropriate because of Nagarjun's vagabond and rather carefree attitude to the affairs of the world, reflected also in his pseudonym 'Yatri' under which he wrote poetry in Maithili.

Accordingly, it is rather ironical that Nagarjun himself has been typecast as a Peoples' Poet, which is nothing but a convenient tool to deflect attention from the complexities and imperfections that his poetry embraced and expressed. In the context of Pablo Neruda, the torch bearer of the poetry of protest in the 20th century, serious attempts have been made to focus on his other aspects, especially the beautiful elemental odes on themes as common place as bicycles, bees, village movie theatre, stamp album, suit, wine etc. to underline his keen observations of daily life. The poems echo what Neruda says in his *Memoirs*: "I am part of the essential majority; I am one more leaf on the great human tree." It is indeed a tribute to the genius of Nagarjun that while carrying the flag of revolution, he showed a deep desire to express, like Neruda, familiar aspects of his rural surroundings by writing poems on and through imagery such as Jack-fruit, twigs of neem tree, chorus of old pair of shoes, cadamba, khichdi, mongoose, roasted corn-cob, little flowers etc. His poem *Jaan Bhar Raheb Hain Jungal Me* (They are Enlivening Up the Forest) celebrates the unmistakable contribution of the 'essential majority' presented in the form of 'numerous glow-worms' who are not to be mistaken as "helpless", instead they are ones who enliven up the entire forest after the rains.

In an article on the Urdu poet Faiz Ahmad Faiz (1911–1984), another flag-bearer of the poetry of protest, and Nagarjun's contemporary who also wrote equally moving personal and sensuous poetry, the eminent theorist of Post-Colonialism, Edward W. Said (1935–2003), imagines Faiz as 'a poet whose poetry combined the sensuousness of Yeats with the power of Neruda'.

Considering that Nagarjun brings with himself a baggage of individual genius that can not fit in any progressive or romantic or modern school of poetry in Hindi literature, he can be compared with Neruda, on the one hand in the manner he juxtaposes the personal with the impersonal and with D H Lawrence, on the other. With Lawrence, more so, for withstanding, albeit like an archetypical outsider, 'the onslaught' of poetic and literary manifestos with personal and literary honesty and a sense of discrimination underlining, like the British novelist, the essential imperfectness of art as its creators themselves are always in the process of evolution.

This essay is a slightly revised version of a radio talk given for the External Service Division of All India Radio in December 2010 on the Occasion of 100th birth anniversary of Nagarjun falling in 2011.

CHAPTER 13

"THE KALEVIPOEG IS MORE AKIN TO OUR DALIT-FOLK-TRIBAL TRADITIONS, THAN THE EPICS"

A Conversation with Vishnu Khare

A conversation with Vishnu Khare (1940–2018), one of our most respected, distinguished and 'enfants terrible', so to say, poet-intellectuals of our times was a matter of pleasure and privilege. The occasion for this conversation, if any occasion was needed at all (since I had the privilege of conversing with him for hours together in person, on phone and mails on a wide spectrum of socio-literary-cultural-personal concerns), was the presentation of the State Decoration of the Order of the Cross of Terra Mariana, IV Class to him as the translator of the Estonian National Epic, *The Kalevipoeg,* by the Honorable Estonian Minister of Education and Research, Mr. Jaak Aaviksoo, on behalf of the President of Estonia, in the presence of the Ambassador of Estonia

H.E. Mr. Viljar Lubi, and many distinguished Indian poets, writers, editors and intellectuals in New Delhi in September 2010.

Before we take the reader into this discussion, it would be interesting to read a passage from the translation shared by Shri Khare with a brief intro. The conversation was conducted through e-mails and telecom.

मृत्यु की बेड़ियों में कलेव पुत्र ने संघर्ष किया
यातना में अपना प्राण-त्याग किया.
खेतों में रक्त जम गया
घटना स्थल को लोहित रँगता हुआ.
उसका शरीर पहले ही कड़ा और ठंढा हो चुका था,
रक्त श्राव शांत हुआ,
उसका हृदय निस्पंद.
तब भी कलेव पुत्र की आँखें
स्वर्ग के पिता के कक्षों की ओर
स्पष्ट दम कर रही थीं,
ऊपर पुरातन पुरुष के आगारों की ओर.

अपने नश्वर बंधनों से मुक्त
उसकी आत्मा उड़ी, एक दीप्तिमान पक्षी की भाँति
वारिदों में विस्तीर्ण पंखों पर,
वह स्वर्ग को आरोहित हुई.
उसकी आत्मा की प्रच्छाया बनने के लिए स्वर्ग में
एक स्वस्थ शरीर को निर्मित किया गया
जो दैवी नायकों की क्रीड़ाओं पर,
गर्जन कारों के भोजों पर,
मधुरतर जीवन का स्वाद ग्रहण करता हुआ
और अपने पार्थिव परिश्रम से विश्राम करता हुआ
अपना हर्षनाद करता था.
वह एक खुले अलाव के पास बैठा,

तारा के नायकों के बीच,
अपना सिर अपने हाथों पर टिकाए हुए,
गायकों के कथाओं को सुनता हुआ;
उसने अपने पार्थिव पराक्रमों को सुना
जीवंत घटनाओं और अचंभों को
अग्नि के पास वार्तालाप में–
चारणों की स्वर्णजिव्ह चर्चा में.

Kumar Vikram:* *Congratulations, Khare Sahab, for this Estonian honour, which I think, is an honour for all Indian poets and translators, and lovers of poetry. We will like to begin from the beginning. How did this project of translating the Estonian Epic *The Kalevipoeg* ***into Hindi come into being?***

Vishnu Khare: Thanks for the kind words, Kumar. As you know, there is a *Sprachbund* called the Finno-Ugric languages and Hungarian, Finnish and Estonian are its major members. Thus there is a strong cultural connect among Hungary, Finland and Estonia. When I was translating such Hungarian poets as Endre Ady, Attila Jozsef, Miklos Radnoti and others into Hindi in the 1980s, the Finnish Literary Society and the Kalevala Society came to know of it and approached me with the proposal that I translate the Finnish national poetic epic *Kalevala*, which runs into nearly 24,000 lines, into Hindi as well. I confessed to them that I did not know any Finno-Ugric language and must translate through the English versions, with occasional help from such mother-tongue experts who had the time and inclination to do so.

To cut a long story short, when the Hindi *Kalevala* was published, for which too I was undeservedly decorated as a

Knight of the White Rose of Finland by the Finnish President, the word went round in the neighbouring Estonia and Ilvi Liive and Kerti Tergem of the Estonian Literary Society and the distinguished Estonian poet Doris Kareva, who met me at the Translators House of NLPVF Holland in Amsterdam, suggested that I took up the translation of their national poetic epic *Kalevipoeg* also, running into nearly 16,000 lines, in Hindi. You see, both *Kalevala* and *Kalevipoeg* have common family-roots and are culturally interrelated. Earlier, I had read the *Kalevipoeg* in a prose-translation. But it was the combined persuasive powers of Ilvi Liive, Kerti Tergem and Doris Kareva that weakened my will and made me take up the back-breaking task. The eponymous hero of the epic is also prone to such rash, near-suicidal misadventures.

KV: What is this epic all about and what way does it stand for the Estonian search for an identity of their own? What was the role of The Learned Estonian Society, Friedrich Robert Faehlmann, and Friedrich Reinhold Kreutzwald in documenting the epic ?

VK: *The Kalevipoeg* begins with the kidnapping of the mother of the rural princely-hero by a rapacious magician – there is this distant echo of the similar kidnapping of Sita in the *Ramayana* - and though Kalevipoeg kills the dastardly villain, he fails to find his mother alive. His heroic father Kalev had already died and must speak to him only from his grave. The "orphan" young man tends to lead an impulsive, complicated life mostly of his own making, kills a few other enemies and demons and some innocent human beings as well but is ultimately immortalised in a strange petrification by the gods-that-be.

It was an article of faith in the entire post-medieval Europe that any country which desired to see itself as a nation ought to have at least one epic of its own. An epicless race was unthinkable – at best a poor relation waiting at the outer portals of the grand European cultural banquet-hall. The Greek and Roman epics did not work – they were a common heritage but there was nothing native about them. Many European countries had their own epics from the pre-Christian, pagan times but not all were so lucky. So anthropologists and ethnographers from such deprived countries began scouring their ancient folk-lore for traces and remnants of narratives which could be rewritten or improvised and claimed as national epics. Both *Kalevala* and *Kalevipoeg*, collected and written by the Finnish Elias Loenrott and the Estonian Friedrich Reinhard Kreuzwald respectively, are direct creative results of this great national urge for an epical identity.

The Platonic institution of "Akademia" was adapted by nearly all European countries as "Learned Societies" catering to their post-renaissance national intellectual or creative pursuits and the Learned Estonian Society was founded for similar objectives in 1838 – it is still active with 114 members - in the university town of Tartu. While the ball for the compilation of *Kalevipoeg* was set rolling by Friedrich Robert Faehlmann in the Learned Society, it was the other member, the aforesaid Friedrich Reinhard Kreuzwald, practising medical doctor by profession and poet, translator, ethnographer-folklorist by choice, who took up the task of creating the *Kalevipoeg* in serious earnest and the first lines of the epic-in-the-making were initially published in the Proceedings of the Society *Oeptatud Eesti Selts* between 1857–1861.

KV: ***Would it be suitable to compare it with the*** *Ramayana* ***or the*** *Mahabharata?*

VK: The protagonist Kalevipoeg seems to me to be a strange combination of Hanuman from the *Ramayana* and Bhima from the *Mahabharata*. Certainly some other parallels could be found – they are found in all epics – but a wholesale comparison would be unjust to both *Ramayana-Mahabharata* and *Kalevipoeg*. The two Indian epics already speak of a comparatively well-developed, near-urban society, more so the *Mahabharata*. The *Kalevipoeg* is an epic of a predominantly rural civilisation – it is basically naive, even innocent. Had there been a pre-Rgvedic epic, it could come close to *Kalevipoeg*. Even our folk-epics are called so because they are composed in folk-dialects – their subject-matter is still mostly feudal. There is also the all-permeating presence of Hindu mythology in its various versions. If narratives from our ancient pre-pagan pre-puranic dalit-folk-tribal traditions could be discovered, collected and recreated, maybe we could have had epics like the *Kalevala* and the *Kalevipoeg*. I am not an expert in ethnography, anthropology or folk-lore and for all I (do not) know, perhaps such epics could still exist. While translating the *Kalevala*, I did hear of a Tulu folk-epic from Karnataka.

KV: Is this epic a living tradition in Estonia—do the young generation identify themselves with the epic in Estonia?

VK: Though not as all-pervasive as the two Indian Hindu epics, which have the dubious advantage of having become semi-religious texts as well, names and motifs from the *Kalevipoeg* are found profusely in modern Estonian literature, drama, music, painting, sculpture and dance. Shops are full of

Kalevipoeg merchandise. The epic has been filmed both for the television and cinema. There are museums devoted entirely or partly to it. Real regions, places and spots are identified with its incidents. Children are sometimes named after its characters. The story has been reworked and retold for children and adolescents. Comics exist. *Kalevipoeg* is present in all curricula, from the primary-school level to the Master's degree. It is a perennial subject of academic research. In any case, that the President of Estonia thinks it proper to bestow a national honour upon a humble Hindi translator of the *Kalevipoeg* from India and his Education Minister himself hands over the medallion to him at the Embassy in the presence of the Ambassador, is surely indicative enough of how seriously the people of Estonia take their epic. But just as the younger generation in India doesn't take its epic-duo frightfully seriously, so also the globalised, Europianised young people in Estonia take their Kalevipoeg with a slight tongue-in-the-cheek combined with a mischievous pinch of salt. But this is perhaps how it should be.

KV: You have been one of our leading modern poets, who has translated a spectrum of modern world poetry into Hindi. How do you respond as a translator to an epic which may not be 'modern' in the sense we understand?

VK: Leading modern poet or not, I do confess that I have translated, perhaps too much, from the so-called world poetry. One of the great advantages we Indians are privileged to have is that we are not compelled only to live in the "modern times". Not only our two epics but hundreds of other ancient books, myths, folk-tales, grandmother-stories resonate in our memory. Then there are the four thousand years old traditions, beliefs, rituals, festivities and superstitions – yes, they as well. Personally, I am reading the *Mahabharata* with an obsessive-manic regularity for the last sixty years and can't have enough of it. I consider Krishna to be the most ideal human being of all times and both Vainamoinen, the "hero" of the *Kalevala*, and *Kalevipoeg* have a touch of the flute-player from Vrindavan. "Modernity" is found in abundance in all great national books and works of art, howsoever ancient they might be. I think it resides in your mind. Buddhism is the most modern faith of them all. Can there be anything more modern than the Rgvedic *Purusha-Sukta*? A strange universality pervades all arts. We have a lot to learn from our own Dalits, village-people and tribes. There are many inspiring passages in the *Kalevipoeg* but the way the hero is maimed by his ambiguous instructions to his own sword and is finally destined to guard forever ossified the gates of the Underworld is as contemporarily relevant as could be.

KV: ***The*** *Kalevputra* ***being a long translation in free verse, how many common readers you think will read it ? Would it not have been more "democratic" to translate it in prose ?***

VK: As a translator, it is my excruciating ambition to be as close to the original as possible, in language, style and craft. Though I had the original *Kalevipoeg* with me all the time, I knew neither the language nor the way to achieve a similar alliteration and rhyme-scheme. You see, translating always helps and inspires a poetaster like me. The best and least I could do was to attempt a free-verse translation in a "literary" register of the language, employed by the great Hindi "Imagist" poets of the 1930–40s. The "heroic" style of Makhanlal Chaturvedi, Ramdhari Singh 'Dinkar' and others was also helpful. But, yes, once this poetic version is sold out, I might think of rewriting the *Kalevputra* as an improvised 'novel', if there is sufficient encouragement. A similar task awaits the *Kalevala* as well. I am convinced that both these "novels" will enjoy a much larger readership in Hindi and in other Indian languages. But I am truly amazed by the enthusiastic responses of the so-called common readers even from the so-called Hindi backwaters to the "poetic" *Kalevipoeg* and *Kalevala*.

The interview was conducted for the author's blog www.aboutreading.blogspot.com and published on the blog on October 29, 2013.[1]

CHAPTER 14

POET MANGLESH DABRAL

And Exploration of the 'Other'

Among the post-Raghuvir Sahay generation of poets, Manglesh Dabral (1948–2020) stands tall as a poet who has consistently been exploring the idea of 'the other' in Indian socio-political discourse as a tool to understand as well as reflect change in his surroundings. It is perhaps the most integral aspect of his poetic journey in which the cross currents of different worlds find a disturbing echo. In fact, for Dabral, coming to terms with the reality of the other is almost akin to coming to terms with himself, with his inner world and his poetic journey seems to be unconsciously working its way onward towards a kind of reconciliation between the two. It is certainly not an easy journey to take, and what separates Dabral from many of his contemporaries, is his ability to reach out to ever-changing distressing realities that lie beyond the boundaries of his daily ambience.

In his first collection of poems *Pahar Par Lalten* (A Lantern on the Mountains, 1981), he has some vague notions of the other in the form of 'his shadow' that automatically becomes 'another person's shadow' in the Section 4 of *Train Me Saat Kavitayen (*Seven Poems in Train, 1977). This vague notion is further concretized when he gets aware of his 'other hand' that is 'almost in disuse', oblivious of the bad world that the main hand encounters day in and day out. It is only when things are stretched a bit far that 'the other hand sometimes registers its protest'. However, this awareness of the other still carries a tone of patronage as the poet believes it 'remains hidden somewhere like a hare in the bush' or 'between ball and the wooden horse of his childhood', perhaps not ready or not meant to engage with the dark realities of life.

This awareness of the silent identity of *Doosra Haath (*The Other Hand), written in 1983 and collected in *Ghar Ka Raasta* (Path to Home, 1988), takes a great leap and in *Sangatkaar* (The Accompanist, 1995), included in *Awaaz Bhi Ek Jagah Hai* (Voice is also a Space, 2000), it gets transformed into a symbol of something of a historical relationship between the dominant and the minor with the experiences of the minor in the focus: *Since long ago/ The resonance of his voice has echoed/The sonority of his master's.*

But the restlessness of Dabral's poetic journey does not allow him to be complacent. The recognition of the silhouetted identity of the other inevitably leads him to a painful understanding of the reasons behind his own backwardness as an individual as well as a social being as he finds he has 'two lives' to handle in a manner in which the success of the one is not dependent on the failure of the other: *Had I only one life I would have reached immediately/ Would have arrived somewhere successfully/-----/But I have two lives to contend with at the same time.* In his perhaps the most mature poem of the later phase 'Two Lives' (*Kathadesh, May 2008)*, we find that the other walks with him on equal footing

> My one hand often pushes some mountain
> With my other hand I hold on to a piece of sky

even though the agonizing dramatization of the poet's situation in these lines makes it a reflection of the forked times that we are living in.

What may appear to be Dabral's temporal and apparently simplistic movement towards the proper understanding of the other is actually a reflection of the revolutionary socio-political changes that have been sweeping the Indian landscape for the last two decades, especially in the North India. A significant poet like Manglesh Dabral, trained under the parameters of the left-liberal poetic dialogue, responds by criticizing the mindless globalization taking place in the society where one day, when humanity loses all its humanness, it will be 'rewarded' with 'the key to a big car and a fat cheque' (*Bhoomandlikaran*, Globalization, *Kathadesh, May, 2008).* He goes further and directly attacks the divisionary tactics of the reactionary forces and leads the secular poetry of protest of our times.

But the problem for Dabral's generation of poets comes when it has to deal with the historical analysis that is brought in by the post-colonial writers in the form of Dalit writings and writings by women. This makes it all too complex, a complexity that was denied to a Muktibodh (1917–1964) or a Raghuvir Sahay (1929–1990)—the pioneers of 'modern' Hindi poetry. It certainly arises out of the clash of 'alternatives' brought about by the economic liberalisation of, by and for the upper middle class, on the one hand, and the rise of the subaltern consciousness forcefully altering the agenda of the socio-political discourse as well as power structure, on the other.

The communal agenda is brought in to create confusion about the terms of these discourses and changes.

In the face of this onslaught, when the majority of the poets of Dabral's generation appear to take the short cuts of uncritical admiration, patronage, or turn inward and start regretting the loss of the so-called tranquil past, Dabral pulls up his socks and makes genuine engagement with the sociology and the psychology of, what many believe, the 'real' poetry of protest. Not only in 'Two Lives', but also in a masterly crafted poem *Chhhuo* (Touch, *Naya Gyanoday,* 2007), we find him reaching out to values and systems, that have been considered 'untouchable': *Do not believe in instructions like 'Please Do Not Touch' or 'Touching Not Allowed'/It is a conspiracy in vogue since time immemorial'.*

The muted, almost sensuous tone of the poem also gets linked up with a range of poems about personal relationships that Dabral has written in abundance but has remained under the shadow of poems that have pronounced social relevance. It is a reflection of Dabral's poetic range that his personal memory, regret, sense of loss and failure allow him to identify with wider human suffering. Such poems abound in his collection *Hum Jo Dekhte Hain* (That Which We See), in particular, where he engages himself with his childhood, the mountains where he grew up, and the pictures of his ancestors that he tries to relate with. Similarly, in his collection *Awaaz Bhi Ek Jagah Hai* (Voice is also a Space), which was noticed for its range of poems on music and musicians, we find that he is capable of relating with the other in some unknown, unseen moments of spontaneous love: *while walking, some one else is found walking along side/and in darkness too an arm appears with love* (*Drishya,* Scenes).

This is a slightly edited version of the booklet on the poet published by Sahitya Akademi for the 'Meet the Author' programme held in May 2008 at India International Centre, New Delhi.

CHAPTER 15

NISSIM EZEKIEL AND DOM MORAES

Negotiating the Idea of Belongingness or 'Where I Am'

In the year 2004 two of the 'original' modern poets of Indian English literature, Nissim Ezekiel (1924-2004) and Dom Moraes (1938-2004), made the final exit out of the theatre of our animate world. For the artist *par excellence* that they were in their own unique and distinct sense, the term final exit is at best a misnomer, but the fact that they no longer breathe the world that we live in can hardly be compensated for. Along with A K Ramanujan these two were often considered the original masters of modern Indian English poetry and with their death, one must say, the 'modern' era of Indian English poetry came to an end.

Both Ezekiel and Moraes started writing in the early 1950s and belonged to the first generation of the post-colonial Indian English poets. They introduced the cosmopolitan, urban and rather seclusive voice (both being born in Mumbai and widely travelled) in Indian English poetry as well as literature *per se*, as opposed to the literature of romantic nationalism witnessed in the pioneers like Toru Dutt, Aurobindo, Sarojini Naidu, etc. They showed that it was genuinely possible for an Indian English poet to have a voice of his own, a voice which need not necessarily emanate from the womb of Indian spiritualism or mysticism but which can actually talk about the boredom, alienation, indifference, lack of communication as experienced and encountered in one's surroundings and the way they make up the persona of the modern man.

However, the similarity between Ezekiel and Moraes as poets and as personalities ends here. While Ezekiel's approach to his poetry as a vocation was rather methodical, Moraes somehow could not shake off the reputation of being someone who wrote poetry by fits and starts.

Moraes was a romantic at heart and so also was his poetry. He remains a veritable outsider whom the question of belongingness plagued throughout his life. Though Ezekiel sorted out the question of belongingness to the country of his birth in the tradition of individualistic-yet-plural Indian ethos, such a finding was almost denied to Moraes. One may say that in the poem titled 'Babur' (From *Later Poems: 1967–1987*) Moraes could finally sort out the question of belongingness in the true fashion of an aesthete, where he says, 'If you look for me, I am not here./ My writings will tell you where I am."

This restlessness of an outlier is expressed by him in many a poem including 'A Letter', included in his *Poems (1960):*

'Almost I can recall where I was born:
The hot verandas where the chauffeurs drowse,
Backyard dominion of the ragged thorn,
And nameless servants in my father's house,

Whispering together in the backyard dirt
Until their talk came true for me one day:
My father hugging me so hard it hurt,
My mother mad, and time we went away.'

This is further explained by him in his autobiography *My Son's Father*:[1]

> 'My mother's parents were both doctors...and Roman Catholics. My paternal grandfather was an engineer, and a Roman Catholic too, but the Hindu caste system of their forefathers had worked on Indian Catholics over the years, splitting them into communities: and my parents' families came from different Catholic communities. A great deal of fuss ensued, but in 1937 my parents married, and on July 19th, 1938, I was born.'

In fact, the two things that have been the highlight of Dom Moraes as writer and as an individual have been underlined by many: his reputation of being an 'outsider', and his poetic sensibility that extends to his prose well. In this context, the other important writer that comes to our mind is the Hindi writer, Nirmal Verma (1929–2005). It would be a good idea to do some kind of comparative analysis of their writings—both being contemporaries, though Verma was a bit senior, and both sort of 'outsiders' to the Indian socio-literary and cultural ethos in their own way.

I tried to probe, and got a feeling that the tag of being an 'outsider', has been used quite indiscriminately for Dom Moraes. Some blame Dom himself would have to take for he seems to have used it to create an aura of mysteriousness around him as reflected in his verse and the titles of his books like *Gone Away, Never At Home, Absences* etc. However, what disturbs me more—and this needs to be evaluated further—is the claim of certain critics that Dom actually hated India. Khushwant Singh, one of the most over-estimated commentators of our times and the perfect practitioner of the art of employing superlative degrees and exaggerations without any qualms, went on to say in his *Tribune* article (*Saturday, October 13, 2007, Requiem to Dom Moraes)*, "He (Dom) disliked everything about India, particularly Indians", adding in good measure, "The only exceptions he made were good-looking women he took to bed." I deliberately quote the second line from that para of Singh, because even in an article written by Geeta Doctor in *The Hindu* on July 14, 2013 under the title 'The Poet Who Remained a Boy', the focal point states, "The greatest asset of Dom Moraes, whose 75th birth anniversary falls on July 19, was his closeness to women and beauty."

My concerns are two-fold: One, this is the way how journalists approach the literary figures and do greatest disservice to the personality as well as to the readers, and secondly, which is more important, is how new generation of readers and critics should make their own assessment of writers or for that matter of any public figure of the times gone by for better understanding of their relevance.

The first concern I am not going to dwell on here because journalistic simplification of literary dilemmas is a deep-rooted disease, and hence I am only leaving it to the judgment of the readers. The second concern I try to address a bit later in the essay after some engagement with Ezekiel's contribution as that would prove to be a good leitmotif to understand the literary and social positioning of Moraes as well.

As compared to Moraes, Ezekiel needed something more concrete to belong to. And his return to India in the 1960s from London emanated from his conviction that he as an artist needs to first belong to the place called India. In this context, the reference to Ezekiel as an 'Indian-Jew' poet sounds strange. After all, do we write Indian-Hindu poet, Indian-Muslim poet and so on and so forth. But one finds this being mentioned at lot of places. May be one needs to read this absolutely fabulous poem of Nissim Ezekiel, arguably the 'father' of modern India-English poetry (will they take the tag back someday?), wherein he explores his Indianness through various images that confront him with his own minor place among the minorities in India. Surely, in the context of Nissim Ezekiel, his placement as an Indian-English writer, a kind of a linguistic minority in Indian literature despite the English language being a tool of the powerful in India, has its own dynamics.

This he conveys in his poem 'Background, Casually' (published in 1976 collection *Hymns in Darkness*, though originally written for a Commonwealth Arts Festival in 1965). The poem, laced with irony and subtle humour, at one level is the inner struggle of a 'mugging Jew' to find his identity in a country of multiple identities, but at the deeper level it underlines that for the poet 'Indianness' is more of a personal discovery from where he can ground himself to have a world-view of his own. The poem ends thus:

I have made my commitments now.
This is one; to say where I am
As others choose to give themselves
In some remote and backward place.
My backward place is where I am

The sheer force of 'Where I am' with which the poem ends also explains the transformation of Ezekiel into a leading light of the movement for bringing recognition to Indian English literature, especially poetry. Actually speaking, what the poem hits at, and this has been one of the influential poems for me to understand and explore one's own position in the time and space that one inhabits, is how the backwardness of one's society, or country is part and parcel of one's own self and identity, and how willy-nilly, both impinge upon each other. Thus, besides being the poet who broke fresh ground, he would always be remembered as one who worked tirelessly and successfully to make people take Indian English poetry seriously. In this phase of life, Ezekiel, the iconoclast, was inspired by nationalistic convictions to establish the identity of Indian English poetry. The poem is also supposed to express the inherent motive of Nissim Ezekiel finally coming back to India from England, and start the complex life of an intellectual in India focussed on finding some space for Indian-English writings, especially, poetry.

In all fairness to the genius of Moraes (whose receiving of Hawthornden Prize for Best Poetry Book in 1957 for *A Beginning* at the age of 19 in London is justifiably now a part of Indian literary folklore), we can say that the 'activist' part of Ezekiel's life had its counterpart in Moraes' contribution to Indian English prose—a prose which is actually an extension of his poetic sensibility as well as diction.

Ironically, for somebody who had the reputation of being a 'stranger', it may be interesting to note that he wrote more books about India than most of the known writers of our times. His travelogues about India like *Gone Away (1960), The Open Eyes: A Joyrney through Karnataka (1974), A Family in Goa, Bombay (1979), Answered by Flutes: Reflections from Madhya Pradesh (1983),* and then his masterpiece *My Father's Son: A Poet's Autobiography (1968), The Tempest Within: An Account of East Pakistan (1971) etc.* also sort of explain comparatively small output of his poetry.

Certainly, the contribution of Moraes to the making of Indian English Literature is purely through written words and his 'writings do tell us where he is'. As a poet, Moraes is more in the company of some of the British poets like W H Auden and Dylan Thomas (who was his friend), as his early poems show him, to quote Bruce King, 'touched by sexual desires, guilt and awareness of his relations with others'. Moraes had a distinct ear for Western music and he utilises it in his poetry admirably well. The first para of his short lyric 'Song' exemplifies the inner discipline in the use of stresses and rhyme:

I sowed my wild oats
Before I was twenty
Drunkards and turncoats
I knew in plenty.
Most friends betrayed me.
Each new affair
Further delayed me.
I didn't care.

Ezekiel and Moraes enriched and moulded Indian English literature in their own ways. Their differing approaches to the question of 'belongingness' will keep providing the artist in India different but equally honest prototypes for negotiating this dilemma.

PERSONAL ESSAYS

CHAPTER 16

THOUGHTS ON A FAMILY-FOLK HERO

Prof. Damodar Thakur

Filial duties can come back to you in various forms. A write-up on Prof. Damodar Thakur (1923–2012) should actually have been written by my father[1]. But since that is not to be; I try to fill in the space. It is rather ironical that while planning a possible book of essays in memory of my father, I came up with a 'wish list' of the scholars who could be requested to contribute to the proposed work. Prof. Damodar Thakur was to be one of the distinguished Advisers of the proposed work. As I have mentioned, this was just a 'wish list', which I shared with my most respected Chacha, my father's elder brother,[2] via an e-mail dated 20th April 2012—nearly 5 months after my father's demise and now almost a year back. Oblivious of all such 'wish lists' and 'planning', Prof. Thakur breathed his last in June 2012 in Benaras. I, of course, had never visualised that I would have the privilege of getting associated with a book of essays being brought out in his memory and honour, being jointly edited by Prof. M M Thakur, brother of Prof. Thakur and Shri S N Sinha, brother of my father, as mentioned.

In an e-mail written after the demise of the grandsire of English scholars, on 9th June 2012 to Prof. Jabir Husain[3], I mentioned the death of Prof. Thakur thus: "With the demise of Prof. Damodar Thakur, one may say that it is now curtains on that glorious era of English scholars from Bihar." Prof. Jabir Husain replied the very next day with these words: "Yes, you are right, Prof Thakur's passing away is a great loss. He was yet another scholar, quietly devoted to studies. I had a personal relationship with him, too. He was our University head at Bhagalpur." Prof. Jabir Husain's reply was just an illustration of the galaxy of students and teachers of English literature, especially in Bihar, who had come in his contact over an active intellectual life spanning perhaps nearly seven decades.

In this context, I may like to mention that my father had this life-long regret of not having the privilege of being taught by Prof. Thakur. He took admission as a post-graduate student in Department of English at L S College, Muzaffarpur in the year 1957 after graduating with English Honours from C M Arts College, Darbhanga, and by that time Prof. Thakur had moved on to Bhagalpur University. Nevertheless, Prof. Thakur remained an integral part of the family folklore and much of it was also due to the special bonding that Shri S N Sinha had shared with Prof. Thakur, besides the regular encounters that my father had with him. Incidentally, one of the usual contexts in which Prof. Thakur's name would crop up in our family discussions related to his insightful observations on the poetry of Shri S N Sinha, who considered Prof. Thakur as his 'first reader' and a positive opinion from Prof. Thakur on any new poetic composition of him, usually meant that the poem had 'passed the muster.'

Fortunately enough, I too had my own share of some interactions and encounters with Prof. Thakur making him a real human being for me away from his folk hero status in our family. I joined the editorial department of National Book Trust, India in March 2000. Perhaps due to my journalistic background and also due to the fact that I had been an English literature student, within a month, I was put into the editorial team of the in-house *NBT Newsletter,* beside the main responsibility of editing and publishing books given to me. For the one full decade I would continue to contribute to the *Newsletter* till 2010 before becoming Senior Editor to be out of the assignment for a younger team to take over. Being a young recruit and with the full support of the then Editor of the *NBT Newsletter*, Ms. Manju Gupta, I could expand the scope of the contents of the *Newsletter* by adding a column of review-cum-interviews of some of the new arrivals of other publishers for the benefit of the readers. Among the people whose addresses I compiled for sending the *Newsletters* included Prof. Damodar Thakur.

Between 2000 and 2004, in particular, I had opportunities to review as well as interact for interviews with writers such as Mrinal Pandey, Amit Chaudhuri, Keki Daruwalla, C D Narasimhaiah, Mohsin Hamid, Sisir Kumar Das, Katherine Frank, B R Nanda, Dipankar Gupta, to name a few, besides reviewing books of Shashi Tharoor, V S Naipaul, Pankaj Mishra, Rajkamal Jha etc and writing pieces on Dom Moraes, Nissim Ezekiel, Premchand, Rajkamal Chowdhary, R K Narayan, Pash etc. Through Shri S N Sinha, I would get the 'feedback' that Prof. Thakur has been receiving the *Newsletters*, and has been quite pleased to read the articles. Naturally, such encouragements for a young reviewer like me provided some kind of intellectual steroids, so to say, to read and write more diligently to keep upto the expectations of the readers which included such distinguished scholars as Prof. Thakur. In fact, after reading the review, titled *Among the Somnambulists,* of the USA-based Pakistani novelist Mohsin Hamid's debut novel *Moth Smoke* and my interview with him, it was a privilege to receive a postcard from Prof. Thakur—his trademark—which we published under the 'Mail Bag' with the editorial sub-heading to the letter 'More on Indo-Anglia'.

Fortunately, I have been able to keep a record copy of the issue concerned (February 2002) and have the pleasure to reproduce the letter:

> *Thank you for sending me the NBT Newsletters. They wake me up to present-day writings. I have missed your interview with C. D Narasimhaiah. How was the interview with Mohsin Hamid conducted? One would like to know a little more about the author so we would place him in some kind of context. I wondered as I read the interview if he had read L. H Myers?*
>
> *Would it be worth digging up old giants/fogeys like Narayan, Anand or Raja Rao just to measure the way things are moving in Indo-Anglia.*
>
> *Patna, Prof. (rtd.) Damodar Thakur*

It was actually a personal letter addressed to me, and when I showed it to the Editor out of excitement, she just took the decision of putting it in the 'Mail Bag' for others to read. I now realise how correct the decision was, because the printed words have their own sanctity, and also because they communicate with a variety of readers in a mysterious fashion. One can't but marvel at the way each and every word is loaded with meaning and insight in the letter. Though it has hardly 90 words, it is amazing to notice the sweep of critical input which it contains, sent through just a post-card. The remarks of Prof. Thakur about Mohsin Hamid have a context and I am reproducing one Q & A out of my interview with Hamid which Prof. Thakur seems to be referring to for the benefit of the readers of this write-up. The interview and the review of *Moth Smoke* were published in July 2001 issue of the *NBT Newsletter:*

> ***The treatment of the story is well crafted. Who/what are your major literary influences?***
>
> The question of literary influence is always a difficult one. I am not sure who they are, only who I would like them to be. Some of the writers I admire most are Nabokov, Camus, Manto, and Borges. Among the living, I enjoy whose names start with 'M', so Morrison, Murakami, Marquez, and Martin Amis. As a child, I was an enormous fan of E B White, Kenneth Grahame, and J R R Tolkien. I also read the 'Choose Your Own Adventure' books. Which of these have most shaped my writing, I have no idea.

Though it is just a matter of pure coincidence but it is really interesting that Prof. Thakur is also asking from Mohsin Hamid about the possible reading of an author whose surname starts with 'M', i.e, Myers! The interview with Mohsin Hamid, on the occasion of the publication of his first novel, a complex modern-day parody of the conflict between Aurangzeb and Dara Shikoh set in contemporary urban Lahore, was conducted via e-mail. I also sent Mohsin Hamid a copy of this issue by post to his New York address so that he could have a look at these comments coming from an Indian scholar, especially because the last line of his interview had stated, "I am looking forward to the messages that are going to come out of Pakistan".

Interestingly, as pointed out earlier about the mysterious fashion in which printed words communicate with the readers, following the publication of Prof. Thakur's letter in the *Newsletter,* I received a letter from Prof. C D Narasimhaiah. I had interviewed him (which Prof. Thakur has mentioned in his letter) in one of the issues on the occasion of the publication of his collection of essays titled *Makers of Indian Literature* and carried its review too.He, too, was an avid reader of the *Newsletter*. Prof. Narasimhaiah sent me an invite to present a paper at a seminar on the role of 'Literary Journals' at his Dhavanyalok centre in Mysore also enclosing a copy of the latest issue of journal *The Literary Criterion* edited by him. Though due to official commitments, I could not avail myself of the opportunity of participating in the seminar, what I remember most is that in that letter, Prof. Narasimhaiah mentioned about the letter of Prof. Thakur published in the previous issue stating that 'I and Damodar were together at Cambridge', which I knew about, but coming directly from him had its own joy.

National Book Trust, India organised the National Book Fair at Gandhi Maidan, Patna from 1–9 December 2001. Alongwith my senior colleague Dr. Devshankar Navin, Hindi editor in the Trust, I was given the responsibility of organising literary programmes at the Fair. The nine-day event had talks and discussions mainly involving some of the stalwarts of Hindi and Urdu literature like Rajendra Yadav, Kedarnath Singh, Uday Prakash, Abdus Samad, Arun Kamal etc. A seminar on 'Impact of Globalisation on Indian Culture' was also planned. I thought that none other than Prof. Damodar Thakur should chair the seminar as he himself was a living legendary symbol of global and Indian culture. I talked over phone to him from Delhi and he promptly agreed.

At Patna, on the day of the discussion, I went to receive him at his Rajendra Nagar residence in an official car. I reached his residence in time, perhaps at 9 AM, as the programme was scheduled for 10 AM. This was my first, and proved to be the only, personal meeting in flesh and blood with the folk hero of my extended family. Prof. Thakur was all dressed up in his characteristic English suit, donning a hat with a stick in his hand. The drive to Gandhi Maidan in the morning hardly took 20 minutes. During the drive, he enquired from me about the focus of the discussion, while adding that 'global' impact on Indian culture has always been there. During the conversation, he also made it a point to personally say that he had been enjoying reading the *Newsletter* and encouraged me to keep writing on. He was also keen to know about the kind of books I edited and published from NBT.

As it were, the punctual and hurried arrival at Gandhi Maidan at around 9.45 A.M proved to be an anti-climax of sorts, because while all the speakers had arrived, there was paucity of audience. Both I and Dr. Navin, being the organisers, became too worried and were placed in an awkward situation. It was all the more baffling because generally the programmes on the other days were having packed crowd. However, Prof. Thakur took it easy and he advised all of us to postpone the programme by an hour saying '10 A.M in winter may be too early for the audience'. We all sat down basking under the winter sun sipping tea. The other speakers, the names of some of whom I am missing, included Hindi poet Madan Kashyap and Maithili writer Ashokji. I remember my colleague Dr. Navin, himself a Hindi-Maithili writer, getting completely bemused when Prof. Thakur and Ashokji got into a conversation in Maithili—Dr. Navin perhaps being unaware about the Maithil antecedents of Prof. Thakur.

The programme started at 11 A.M when the audience started trickling in and very soon we had a good audience of nearly 150. While some of the speakers underlined the disturbing impact of globalisation on Indian culture and society, Prof. Thakur had a word of advice to offer when he gave the presidential address. I had reported about the activities of the Patna Book Fair in the *NBT Newsletter*, which was published in the January 2002 issue, and I would like to reproduce from it the relevant passage:

> In the second[4] seminar on 'Impact of Globalisation on Indian Culture', a lively debate followed. While some speakers bemoaned the damaging Western influences on Indian psyche, others found it a manifestation of inferiority complex. In his presidential lecture, eminent scholar of English literature, Prof. Damodar Thakur pointed out that "the influence of the Western culture can be resisted if we have high self-esteem and learn to have faith in our own culture and tradition."

Though Prof. Thakur had agreed to speak in Hindi at the seminar considering the largely Hindi-knowing composition of the audience at the Fair, but ultimately he opted to speak in English, which, as Shri S N Sinha, later aptly put it, was 'his natural disposition.' The Patna Book Fair provided me rare opportunities to share dais with a galaxy of litterateurs including Prof. Thakur.

On the way back to drop him at his residence, the journey was unusually long and tedious because we apparently got caught in the afternoon traffic of school buses. Nonetheless, the longish duration of Prof. Thakur's august company resulted in fruitful discussions. It so happened that those days in 2001–02, I was busy planning a book of critical essays titled *Aspects of English Literature* to be written by different Indian scholars. I had discussed the project with Ms. Kalpana Rajaram, Editor and Publisher of Spectrum Books Pvt. Ltd, New Delhi. In fact Spectrum publishing house had provided me my first job in 1996, and later published my first book *Short Essays* in 2002. Also, between 1997 and 2003, my father and I co-authored *T S Eliot: An Intensive Study of Selected Poems*[5] for

Spectrum which was ultimately published in 2005. In fact, in this backdrop, Ms. Rajaram agreed to be the co-editor with me for the collection of essays, and we wrote to good number of professors across India requesting them to contribute to the volume and procured the same from many of them. My father also wrote five essays for the volume, one of which titled 'Approaches to Shakespeare', was based on his lecture given at the Academic Staff College Refresher Course for English Lecturers organised by B R A Bihar University some time back. On that particular day of our journey back to Rajendra Nagar from Gandhi Maidan, I requested and impressed upon Prof. Thakur to contribute one or two essays to the volume. I somehow could also convey that eminent professors like him should contribute more by writing for the posterity. Prof. Thakur smiled and said that he had been taught by eminent professors like Prof. Amarnath Jha, 'who never wrote a single line', as he put it. There were great professors like Prof. F Rahman, Prof. Mahendra Pratap, who also did not give much importance to writing, he said, adding, 'actually we believed in giving everything in classrooms to the students'. This line of argument was not new for me for my father himself believed in and followed it. However, Prof. Thakur did say that 'some amount of writing should be done', and agreed to look into the possibility of contributing an essay or two to the proposed volume mentioned by me.

Back to Delhi, some months later, I sent him a list of probable essays that he could take up. He chose 'Intention and Idiom of Modern Poetry' and one more topic, which I am unable to remember, more so, because while Prof. Thakur sent us a full length essay on the first one, his second essay came to us in the form of some points which he thought he would be able to develop further later on. I was particularly happy that he chose the topic, which I can take the credit of coining taking a cue from Ian Jack's study titled *Augustan Satire: Intention & Idiom in English Poetry 1660–1750.* When my father learnt about the topic chosen by Prof. Thakur, he remarked, 'It is good because only he could have done justice to the topic.' The handwritten essay arrived sometime in October 2003. It is datelined '*Wedneday 17 July 03*', the signature of Prof. Thakur at the end of the essay has '*14/09*' as the date. Apparently the writing of the essay extended from 17 July to 14 September 2003. The essay is comprehensive in its conciseness, and being a part, even though, insignificant, of the process leading to the writing of the essay, I feel like reproducing a para from it as being probably one of the first readers of the essay:

> No modern poet can consent to write in the poetic diction of another period, however strongly and vitally that poetic diction may speak to him in his own literary, cultural sensibility. If the play with language which is so vital a part of the creativity of language; which is the creativeness of a poet's work, has already been performed by another poet and another time, no modern poet can accept it as genuine poetic action in his own work.

In between, Shri S N Sinha also gave me a set of poems of Prof. Thakur, which contained some of his original poems in Hindi, English and Maithili, a few translations of French poems into Maithili. The idea, of course, was to read, and then to try for their publications at appropriate platforms. Somehow, I could not get them published.

Perhaps, my last interaction with Prof. Thakur through letters[6] was sometime in 2009, when I received a post-card from him requesting to buy through VPP a copy of Mohit Sen's *Autobiography* published by[7] National Book Trust, India in 2007. Courtesy Shri S N Sinha, I was aware about Prof. Thakur's famed friendship with Mohit Sen, he having also referred to Prof. Thakur in his autobiography. I sought permission to officially send him a complimentary copy of the book underlining the fact, and was promptly granted the same. While sending him the copy, I, for good measure, suggested to him that an eminent scholar like him should also think about penning down his memoirs. He wrote back to say that he would try. It is learnt that he did write a few pages on his relationship with Mulk Raj Anand, but I am afraid that the pages are not traceable.

I take the opportunity to reproduce a brief extract from Mohit Sen's book wherein he mentions Prof. Thakur in order to illustrate not only their friendship, but, in turn, their association with another illustrious personality called E M Forster. To quote from para four of the chapter 3 titled 'In Cambridge', p. 47–48:

> ...As I was walking in the great first quadrangle of King's, a slightly bent old spectacled man walked past, looked at me, walked on and then turned back. He said that, surely, I was from India and added 'I am Morgan Forster'. I was taken aback, shook his hand and accepted his offer for tea in his room in the College. I had read E. M. Forster's *Howards End* and *A Passage to India* while in India. On board the *Maloja* on my way to England, Damodar Thakur, who was coming up to read English at St. John's in Cambridge, had given me a copy of Forster's *What I Believe.* I had been both impressed and irritated by the booklet.

While Mohit Sen goes further to talk about his interactions with Forster at Cambridge, in the context of reference to Prof. Thakur in the ambience of the talk about Forster, it may be worthwhile to also mention Prof. Thakur's own relationship with E. M Forster. Since this was a glorious part of the family folk tales related to Prof. Thakur with Shri S N Sinha being the chief narrator of the same,

I have the temptation of combining all these associations—that of Forster's with Prof. Thakur and of Prof. Thakur's with Shri S N Sinha— because there is a readymade connection available.

In his highly perceptive essay titled 'Breaking New Grounds' on Shri S N Sinha's first poetry collection in Hindi titled *Aathwan Din*,[8] Prof. Thakur elucidates the central intention of the collection through the following illustration:

> A week has seven days. We speak of five-day weeks, hopefully, in other places, even of four-day weeks. The eighth day is outside the frame. This selection of poems is called *Aathwan Din*, a day that is outside the frame-work of time, a day that does not exist in the calendar. A title is not a poem, but it is an indication of the thought and attitude of the poet, of the inwardness and subtlety of language that is part and parcel of the poems themselves. I am reminded of a painting by Jamini Roy which E. M Forster showed me in his London flat which had a lovely blue Krishna playing the flute. The strange thing was that some of the wavy hair of Krishna and all the peacock feather were above the topline (a part of the painting itself and not the wood frame). Like the eighth day of the week.[9]

I, too, have special connection with these lines. First, because I have read the poems of *Aathwan Din* many a time and also wrote its review and this illustration instantly provided an insight that a reader-reviewer of the poetry collection could utilise as per his/her perceptions and orientations. Secondly, on a broader note, such realised statements come handy in numerous ways to negotiate various situations of life.

For example, I had an opportunity to organise the book release function of Prof. G P Pradhan[10]'s eminently acclaimed Marathi political novel translated into English under the title *A Tale with Seven Answers*[11] published under my editorial supervision by NBT.

The release function was organised at Pune to commemorate the birth anniversary of Pradhan in August 2011 in collaboration with the Department of English, University of Pune. The book was translated by Prof. Shrikant Tambe, a retired professor of English from Aurangabad, and released by Shri Kumar Ketkar, eminent journalist and editor, with a special paper by eminent Marathi critic, Prof Arun Sadhu. As it happens, the discussion turned to the role of literature in human society. I utilised the above lines of Prof. Thakur to illustrate a point while summing up the discussions. I remember a few from the audience walking upto me appreciating the reference to Prof. Thakur, E M Forster and Janimi Roy's painting in the context of the discussion.

When I lost my father in November 2011, I received a message from Prof. Thakur through Shri S N Sinha stating that 'please convey to him whatever you can on my behalf at this hour.' I can only say that rather intermitten interactions with Prof. Thakur over a period of one decade or so, while having grown up on the stories and anecdotes related to him in the extended family during my childhood and growing up years, provided valuable learning which would help keep one intellectually committed, as well as grounded.

The article was included in the Commemmorative Volume published on Prof. Damodar Thakur in 2014 (Edited by M. M. Thakur et al), Darbhanga, Bihar.

CHAPTER 17

POST-COLONIALISM AS A WAY OF LIFE

Biography of an English Professor-Activist

Arun Kumar Sinha (27 August 1940–28 November 2011) was a Professor in English at Langat Singh College (established in 1899), B R A Bihar University, Muzaffarpur, Bihar, India, from where he retired as its Principal in the year 2000. [1] An acclaimed social activist, one of the important pillars of Teachers' Movement, especially in North Bihar, and a committed teacher, he is known for his work on T S Eliot and Mark Twain, on the one hand, and his role and contribution to the Socialist and Sarvodaya Movement, on the other. He was also Convener, State Intellectual Cell of Bharatiya Lok Dal, Bihar in the 1980s, and a Member of its State Executive in 1980s, which was led by Chowdhary Charan Singh, a former Prime Minister of India, at the national level. Prof. Sinha was the elected President of L S College Teachers' Association for four times in the 1980s and 1990s and was twice elected General Secretary of the Combined

Teachers' Association of L.S. College and Bihar University PG Departments' College and University Teachers in the early 1980s. In the 1980s and 1990s he served as the Chief Editor of the L S College Magazine 'Vaishali'. He was my, and my elder brother, Kumar Vivek, and elder sister, Vatsala Sinha's father.

Birth, family and influences of his father

Prof. Sinha was born at village Saramohanpur in Darbhanga district, in north Bihar to Shri Bam Bahadur Lal Verma (1894–1962) and Smt Parekhan Devi (perhaps six years younger to her husband, she passed away in 1969) as the youngest child among six brothers and three sisters (a twin sister-brother, however, passed away due to Tuberculosis in early 1940s when Prof. Sinha was hardly a few years old). His father was a multi-faceted personality, whose commitment to education with a rebellious streak, left a mark on all his children, including the youngest one. It may be necessary to refer to an article published posthumously in the Hindi daily '*Navrashtra*' on Shri Bam Bahadur Lal Verma, written by his third son, Shri Badri Narayan Sinha (4th April 1930- 7th November 1979), an officer of Indian Police Service (1952 batch, Bihar Cadre), and an eminent poet-critic of his time, so as to understand the kind of father that Prof. Sinha had which actually provided him the essential training and commitment to life, education, and society.[2]

Early education and career

During his childhood, Sinha was taught by his father at his village home only, and it was only when he turned 11 that he was taken by his father to Marwari High School, Darbhanga for admission in class 9th. Considering the age of Sinha, the school authorities were not keen on giving him admission in such a high class; however, on the insistence of his father the teachers took Sinha's test of English grammar, translation, prose writing and arithmetic. Finding Sinha's understanding of these subjects quite satisfactory, he was granted admission in 9th class. Thus, when in 1953, Sinha matriculated, he was hardly nearly 12 and half years old. He took admission in C M Arts College, Darbhanga in Intermediate Arts (I.A). After passing out from I.A in 1955, he took admission in English Honours in the same college, and graduated with Honours in 1957. In 1957, he moved to Langat Singh College, Muzaffarpur, to pursue post-graduation in English Literature.

However, when in 1959, he took his MA exams, he dropped out after writing only four papers. The fourth paper was 'Essay Paper', in which the student had to write a full length essay on a given subject. He would repeatedly narrate the sequence of events leading him to drop out. In the Essay Paper, he chose to write on 'Treatment of Hell in English Literature'. He thought that he would touch upon the classical literature like Homer's Odyssey, come down to Shakespeare and Dante, and while touching upon neo-classical and romantic age, he would wind up with Eliot's 'The Waste Land' and Modern literature. However, after writing full four pages, he thought that he was not able to handle the topic well. He left midway. Scared that since his one paper had not gone well, he decided to drop out of the exams and attempt to clear MA the next year. He, however, always regretted the decision. He secured 56 marks in that half written Essay paper of 1959, ironically the similar marks that he got in the Essay Paper when he completed his MA in 1960 exams.

Prof. Sinha always stated that perhaps his being just 18+ at that time impacted his rather immature decision to drop out.

It so happened that during that intervening period, the job situation became suddenly tough. While all those who passed out in 1959, generally got lectureship in good colleges, Prof. Sinha had to first join Pandaul College, Madhubani as a temporary lecturer in 1960. From there, he moved to a college in Narkatiyganj, again as a temporary lecturer, before getting a permanent lectureship in M J K College, Bettiah. However, after teaching there for six months, Prof. Sinha moved to M S College, Motihari as a Lecturer in English, joining on 5th December 1961.

Refusal to join Indian Foreign Service (Allied) Prof. Sinha got an appointment to Indian Foreign Service (Allied) in 1964 through the civil service examination conducted by Union Public Service Commission. However, he was desirous of joining Indian Administrative Service. Moreover, Indian Foreign Service (Allied) appointment would have taken six years to get upgradation as Class I IFS. Prof. Sinha, being more than satisfied with teaching career, refused to join the IFS (Allied), even though by the time of retirement the service would have given him minimum three postings as an Ambassador of India.However, Prof. Sinha never regretted his decision not to join IFS, more so, because he was more oriented towards working for his immediate surroundings and the life and career of a diplomat was hardly the one that he craved for. The fact that he never thought of availing himself of another opportunity (he still had one attempt left) to 'clear' civil service shows how satisfied and happy he was in the academic field.

Marriage

Sinha got married to Smt. Kamla Sinha, BA (1964) in 1966. Smt. Kamla Sinha (b. 1942) is the fifth daughter of the noted advocate and freedom fighter Shri Baldeo Narayan (1900–1985) of Samastipur, Bihar. Shri Baldeo Narayan had worked closely with Dr. Rajendra Prasad, the first President of India, during national movement, especially during non-cooperation movement of 1922–23, and

Civil Disobedience Movement of 1930s, launched by Mahatma Gandhi. Shri Naryan was also President of Samastipur Congress Committee during pre-indepedence days, and was closely associated with the Theosophical Society's programmes and activities. His only son, Dr. B N Prasad, was one of the most eminent physicians of Samastipur. Incidentally, Smt. Kamla Sinha was the first female graduate of her family in 1964.

General evaluation of his work

During Prof. Sinha's Principalship, L. S. College also celebrated a part of its centenary year (1999–2000). It may be worthwhile to mention that Government of India is considering to declare the college a heritage monument. [3] Meanwhile, writing about his stint as Principal of Langat Singh College, Prof. Nandkishore Prasad Sharma, himself a former Principal of the College, stated in his book on Langat Singh, the founder of the College, on the occasion of the centenary year celebrations of the college:

> Prof. Arun Kumar Sinha took over as the Principal of the college on 3rd January 2000. Sinha Sahab is a scholar of English, amiable, soft-spoken and social-thinker. The work is going on positively. The renovation work of the college building is progressing with the help of the state government. Our heartiest wishes are with him.[4]

Later in his career, Prof. Sinha wrote a fine longish nearly 100 page introduction to *Huckleberry Finn*[5] and did an Intensive Study of T S Eliot,[6] both published as books by Spectrum Books, New Delhi, the first one with the text of the novel. He co-authored the Eliot book with me, his son. He wrote on long poems like *The Waste Land*, *Ash Wednesday* and also 'Ariel Poems', while his son wrote on *Prufrock* volume and *POEMS: 1920* volume, *The Hollow Men.* The 85 page Introduction was largely by him. It is nearly 500+ pages one of its kind study with intensive annotations and critical essays on individual poems written over a period of 6–7 years published so elegantly by Madam Kalpana Rajaram, Editor and Publisher of Spectrum.

Prof. Sinha also translated the monograph of Ramdhari Singh Dinkar from Hindi to English with many long passages in verse from Dinkar for Sahitya Akademi–published by the Akademi to commemorate the birth centenary year of Dinkar in 2007.[7]

His unpublished works include a full-length intensive study of 'Four Quartets', a novel in English, many critical essays, socio-political writings etc.

Idealist, Rebellious and Down-to-Earth

He had imbibed that true and complex spirit of the 60s–idealist, rebellious, down-to-earth (almost throughout his life he would spend an hour or so in the kitchen garden tending plants) and carrying that streak of detachment—that made him decide not to finish his doctorate on Dylan Thomas, the same streak that made him decide not to join Indian Foreign Service (Allied) on selection in 1964, among many other things, that we would generally be tempted to cling on to. The obituary report titled 'Contributions of ex-principal recalled', published in *The Times of India*, Patna edition on 30 November 2011 stated, among other things, that

> 'Sinha was fondly remembered as principled, committed teacher, social activist, Gandhian and an exemplary human being'.[8] Another leading national Hindi daily 'Dainik Jagaran' called him 'a scholar of English and a thinker'. [9]

Distaste for 'Hero-Worship' and 'Personality-Cult'

Prof. Sinha was born and brought-up in the Nehruvian-era, but under the influence of the Socialist questioning of the era. Nehru was a cult figure and the established political and intellectual class worshipped him like a hero. Almost as a reaction to it, and under the influence of the critical enquiry of the Nehruvian era by stalwarts such as Acharya Narendradev, Ram Manohar Lohia and Jayaprakash Narayan, on the one hand, and the training of intellectual detachment imbibed from the study of English literature, Prof. Sinha came to detest anykind of 'vyakti pooja' or 'hero-worship' or the 'cult of personality'. At the highest level, this was evident in the manner he read and admired even the philosophy of Buddha, Marx, and Gandhi keeping his own individual skepticism intact. Hence, as it were, alongwith Buddha, there always was the Vedantist philosophy of Vivekananda as a parallel text to read, with Marx, a Gandhi was always there as a 'counter-text', with Gandhi, there always was an Ambedkar to contend with, with Nehruvian Socialism, there was the Socialist ideals of Acharya Narendradev, Rammanohar Lohia, and JP to provide an inclusive and critical perspective. No wonder, on the more practical level, this meant that he could never bring himself to admire uncritically the political leaders with whom he worked or others whom he came across. Thus, even among the anti-establishment socio-political parties and platforms, he remained on the other side of the fence to the 'established' power structures of these organisations.

A "Post-Colonial" approach to life and teaching

While in the fields of teaching of English literature as well as research, post-colonial approach has become the watch word during the past three decades or so in India, but for Prof.Sinha post-colonialism was a way of life. Rather it defined his persona and his world view from which emanated his attitudes to life, in general, and to teaching, in particular. To begin with, alongwith the reading of English literary texts, he continued to read and also impressed upon his students to read contemporary Hindi or Urdu literature too. Despite being a teacher of English, he made it a point to send his children to Hindi-medium government-run schools. He found himself closer to that great line of teachers like Prof. Amarnath Jha, Prof. Damodar Thakur, Prof. Kamta Charan Srivastava, Prof. Mahendra Pratap, Prof. H R Ghoshal and many such stalwarts in Bihar, who read and researched throughout their lives not from the perspective of adding the 'list of publications' to their CVs, but only to give their best, deliver almost with religious sincerity, their knowledge, understanding and interpretations of literary texts in the classrooms for the benefit of their students. No wonder, Prof. Jabir Husain, his fellow-traveller in social activism, former Chairperson of Bihar Legislative Council, noted Urdu-Hindi writer and a former Professor of English who studied at L S College in the 1960s, wrote after his demise to his son in response to an article on Prof. Sinha,

> Your father, whom you have rightly introduced in your blog, was one person whom I respected most for his profound scholarship and unassuming nature. I always ranked him with my teachers, Prof KC Shrivastav, Prof HR Ghoshal and Prof DN Mallik, all such persons that have greatly contributed to my life and career.[10]

Actually, Prof. Sinha's general refrain was that a teacher must be able to 'stimulate' the minds of the students. For him, that was the most enlivening ideal for a teacher, much more than his acquiring of degrees or fellowships or scholarships. Teaching was a life-long commitment, a socio-political commitment, so to say, and any teacher's knowledge or research was good enough only if it got delivered effectively in the classroom lectures and the students got benefited out of that. It was this idealism and commitment that goaded him to continue teaching passionately despite the overall deteriorating standard of higher education in Bihar, especially in the later part of his career, when the professors taught without getting paid for months. Whereas a good number of professors in Bihar in the 1990s sought assignments in foreign universities, especially in the middle east region countries like Yemen, Oman, UAE etc, which was quite understandable considering the suffocating– intellectually as well as financially– environment on the campus in the 1990s, Prof. Sinha steadfastly continued to put all his energies and expectations, much to his own personal and intellectual stress, in teaching students of English literature who were mostly drawn from the rural areas of North Bihar.

Prof. Sinha negotiated with the dilemma of committed teaching in the midst of deteriorating standards of higher education in Bihar's educational campuses at various levels. Many a time, he organised meetings, observed dharnas, undertook fasts to bring the attention of the authorities to improve academic environment on the campus. At the same time, he saw to it that at the personal level, he taught honestly, reaching college to take classes on time, and discouraging students to take paid private tuitions from college professors–a 'virtue' which sounds so unfortunately because of the rampant prevalence of such a practice all around him. The students and even his junior colleagues always had free access to him to consult on matters of literary texts without him 'charging' for any such 'consultations'. On the other hand, he always considered himself just a 'student' of literature and not its 'scholar'.

Elucidating this, Prof. Anisur Rahman, Professor of English, Jamia Millia Islamia, New Delhi, and a former student of Bihar University in the 1970s, wrote about one of his encounters with

Prof Sinha in the late 1970s while Prof. Rahman was a Research Scholar with the Department of English, L S College, Muzzafarpur:

> 'Let me tell you of one particular event. Arun Babu had to teach a poem. He started talking to me about that poem. As he shared his reading with me, he also sought my response to that text. Not that I could do anything worthy of mention, but I was humbled by his humility. (Remember he was a faculty member of several years standing and I was a research scholar who had just started). This was a gesture that made me think and I could understand in what different ways this great virtue called 'humility' can be put into practice in this life of ours which is full of pride and conceit. This moment has stayed back with me. I practice it in my own teaching-learning process. And I'm proud that Arun Babu taught me this.' [11]

Two relevant anecdotes: In this context, it may be worthwhile to mention two anecdotes from Prof. Sinha's life, which tell a lot about his personality and his committed approach to work, where idealism merges harmoniously, almost anonymously, with day-to-day practicalities.

Once a Dalit lady was appointed as a Lecturer in one of the departments of Prof Sinha's own college, L S College. Being a bastion of the so-called forward castes, a lot of hue and cry and misinformation campaign was launched against her by the vested interest groups calling her below merit and inefficient. Prof. Sinha, being a respected teacher as well an active Teachers' Association member, always argued in her favour in meetings, get-togethers and informal conversations. However, taking a cue from the vested interest groups, students would generally not allow the concerned Lecturer to take classes peacefully, booing her and creating nuisance. It so happened that once while Prof. Sinha was engaging a class of English Honours, the noise coming from the neighbouring classroom was disturbing him and his class. He immediately dashed into the neigbouring room and found that it was the class of that lady Lecturer with students making fun of her and booing. Prof. Sinha entered the classroom and suddenly there was complete hush and silence. He looked at the Lady teacher and requested her to 'carry on'. He himself did not reprimand the students, but only stood silently for a few minutes almost like a moral force. Being a very senior Professor, no student tried to create any disturbance, even when he left the classroom to carry on with his own class. This act was actually repeated by him on two-three occasions. Gradually, the Lady teacher gained in confidence and learned to handle unruly students and the students too realized their mistakes by and by.

Another anecdote is about a poor student who wanted to take tuitions from Prof. Sinha. Prof. Sinha rarely did private tuitions—and if at all he ever did so, that was only due to long periods of non-payment of salaries or long periods of strikes, which were becoming a norm on the campus. But he was always available to teach students free-of-cost. However, this student, even though quite poor, was not ready to take tuitions without paying him anything. It was a strange dilemma for Prof. Sinha because he also perceived that the student did not seem to be in any condition to pay him and only out of a heightened sense of self-respect he insisted on paying. Prof. Sinha found a way out. The student was a Muslim and knew Urdu. Prof. Sinha sort of struck a deal with him saying that after giving him English tuitions every evening or whenever he happened to visit, Prof. Sinha would like to learn Urdu from him. The student was at first taken aback but happily agreed for the deal. Hence, one could see this unique scene on occasions, when the student after taking lession in English from Prof. Sinha, would spend some time to teach him Urdu alphabet. This way Prof. Sinha could negotiate a dilemma of not taking money from the student while at the same time respecting his sense of self-respect.

Socio-political activism and commitment

His post-colonial rebellious streak also took him to social activism. Despite the reservations which many teachers of English, in particular, and others had regarding Prof. Sinha's penchant for socio-political work, he continued to contribute intellectually as well as 'physically' in that arena. That sometime brought him to the distribution of political pamphlets, pasting of posters in the middle of nights, and also selling of his socio-political periodicals like *Samadhan*, *Chingaari*, *Yuva Jagaran* etc with his associates and students at the railway stations, main markets, residential areas etc. But here also, he remained a sort of an outlier. Coming from the apparently 'elite' class with an English literature background, his championing of the cause of the marginalised and the depressed classes from the Socialist and Sarvodaya standpoint was viewed with suspicion by the leaders of these classes, and while many of his 'followers' went on to reach state assemblies and also the Parliament of the country, his 'clean, no-nonsense and intellectual style politics' pushed him onto the margins, despite working very closely with the likes of Lohia, JP, George Fernandes, Charan Singh, Karpoori Thakur etc. He realised it all, saw it through but could not change his style. He would smilingly say, 'people consider me a holy cow, who needs to be worshipped but not to be followed'.

Sinha, early on his life, got influenced by Communist Movement in the country and joined Communist Party of India in early 1960s. However, soon after, he found the Communist ideology too limiting in the Indian scenario, especially due to the unique conflict that caste-ridden Indian society faced. Sinha, under the influence of both Marx and Gandhi, found the Socialist ideology of Acharya Narendra Dev and Rammanohar Lohia as the most suitable to understand as well as work for an equitable society in India. Delivering his first address from a public platform in 1967 at a mass meeting at Darbhanga presided over by Shri Rammanohar Lohia, Prof. Sinha soon carved a niche for himself, joining anti-Congress forces. At Motihari, he organised agitations as well as seminars against the Brahaminical symbol of *Yagyapawit* (Janeyu) in the 1960s. Also, he not only steered clear of the organisations like 'Chitragupta Associations', he publicly campaigned against such outfits. Toeing the line of his father, he never performed, nor he inculcated among his children, the 'puja' of 'Kalam-Dawaat' on the occasion of Chitragupta Puja considering it tokenism of the highest order in the name of knowledge and learning and completely casteist.

In fact, one of his diary entry states that while a kind of political consciousness was always there in him, he became intensely aware of it and his social responsibility after the tragic incident of police firing on the students and lecturers of R D S College, Muzaffarpur in 1967, when a few students and one lecturer got killed in the same. Anirudh Prasad's study titled *University Education, Administration and the Law*, aptly captures the deeply disturbing scenario of the college and university campuses with reference to this incident of 1967:

> The Police firing at RDS College, Muzaffarpur, which caused death of one Professor and one student, resulted upsurge at Muzaffarpur, Patna, Ranchi, Arrah and other places. It resulted into mob-violence at Patna on 5.1.1967. Students attacked police which fired 55 rounds, result being the loss of life of 9 and injury of 46, mostly the students. It provoked mass protests against the Chief Minister K.B. Sahay

> (and) on 6.1.1967 at 5.15 p.m, about 10,000 students crowd (sic) gathered near Gandhi Maidan Bus Depot after setting fire at many places. The student mob made bid to enter bus department yard. Police had to open fire on the violent mob and as a result 10 persons were killed and 57 were injured. It resulted into the closing of Colleges and Universities for two months.[12]

One may say that the incident left an indelible impression on Prof. Sinha who found, as it were, the right impetus to be a committed and socially awakened teacher.

During the 1974 Jayprakash Movement in Bihar which soon spread all over India, [13] Sinha became the founder-member of the Motihari District Co-ordination Committee formed to carry forward the agitational and awareness programmes related to the 1974 movement. Moving on to Muzaffarpur in 1975, he became one of the key campaigners of electoral success of George Fernandes who fought the historic 1977 Lok Sabha elections from Muzaffarpur constituency from jail. In the 1980s and the 1990s, students from all streams—from SFI, IPF, Chhatra Janata, Chhatra Yuva Sangharsh Vahini, AIDSO and also, sometimes, ABVP and never from NSUI—kept coming to him for guidance and kept inviting him for lectures in their conventions, meetings etc. Through organisational elections, he became a Vice-president of the Muzaffarpur District Lok Dal, and later assumed charge as the Working President. He was appointed as state convener of Bihar Lok Dal's Intellectuals' Cell, as well as Member of its State Executive in early 1980s. This was at a time when the present Chief Minister of Bihar, Shri Nitish Kumar, was the President of Yuva Lok Dal; and the former Chief Minister Shri Lalu Prasad Yadav, as a young MLA of the party, had paid a visit to Prof. Sinha's house as an emissary of Chowdhary Charan Singh, to thank him for organising a successful public meeting in

Muzaffarpur in 1980 for Chowdhary Charan Singh, the President of Lok Dal and a former Prime Minister of India. During this period, Prof. Sinha was comrade-in-arms with leaders like Shri. Ram Vilas Paswan, Shri. Manjay Lal, Shri. Hind Kesari Yadav, Shri. Ram Sanjivan Singh etc.

At Muzaffarpur, besides George Fernandes, some of the political leaders and activists of the left-oriented and of Janata Pariwar who worked very closely with Prof. Sinha included Shri Suresh Achal, Shri Kamal Paswan (later an MLA in Bihar), Dr. Ramchander Purbe (for fifteen years Education Minister under Chief Minister Shri. Lalu Prasad Yadav and Smt. Rabri Devi), Shri Anand Bhushan (Lok Dal leader), Prof. Shailendra Nath Shrivastava (worked eminently for Literacy Mission in Muzaffarpur), Shri Nalini Ranjan Singh (SUCI MLA from Kanti), Shri Arun Kumar Singh (State Secretary, SUCI), Shri Harender Kumar (later an MLA and then President, Chhatra Janata), Captain Jainarayan Singh 'Nishad' (later Lok Sabha MP), Shri Vinod Prasad Singh (ex-MLA), Prof. Ragahav Prasad (ex-MLA and ex-State President of Lok Dal) etc.

On his death, Sinha was remembered as a 'thinker of Socialist ideology', who 'contributed significantly to the political work of leaders like Dr. Rammanohar Lohia, Jayprakash Narayan, Chowdhary Charan Singh and Karpoori Thakur'. [14]

Appointment as Proctor, L S College, Bihar University, and Resignation in Protest

In 1981, while Prof. Sinha was still an elected General Secretary of the Combined Teachers' Association of L S College and Bihar University P G Department Faculty members, a very strong body, and virtually the representative of the voice of the college and university teachers of the North Bihar, he was appointed as Proctor to L S College, Bihar University by the Vice-Chancellor, Prof. Shyam Nandan Kishore to improve and maintain the overall academic environment on the campus and to aid and advice the administration on the same. Since as the General Secretary, Prof. Sinha had been in the forefront to raise issues related to maladministration on the campus, he readily gave his consent to be a Proctor as offered by the Vice-Chancellor. It was indeed a ticklish situation, to be part of administration as well as being a General Secretary of the Teachers' Association, still Prof. Sinha agreed to be a Proctor in order to walk the talk. Moreover, Prof. Sinha had the greatest tradition of Proctorship in mind when publicly prominent members of teaching profession of an educational institution are appointed to positively influence the agenda of the administration for the greater common good.

However, it so happened that when the formal notification for his appointment as a Proctor was issued, it also stated that he would be paid 'honorarium' for the Proctorship. Prof. Sinha took a strong exception to it because when the informal offer was made by the University Administration, there was no mention of any extra honorarium to be paid for the assignment. Prof. Sinha resigned in protest, while stating that he saw no reason why there should be any extra payment involved for Proctorship, when he was already drawing salary as a Lecturer and he considered it his bounden duty to work for the improvement of academic atmosphere on the campus. He quit mentioning that the notification had caused 'embarrassment' to him. In order to make the protest as one of dignity of the teachers *per se*, he used the letter head of the 'Bihar University Teachers' Association' and signed as its General Secretary. The text of the resignation letter is reproduced herewith.

TEXT OF THE RESIGNATION LETTER

10 September '81

To
The Vice-Chancellor,
Bihar University, Muzaffarpur

Sir,

This relates to the formation of the Proctorial Board for L S College and my appointment to the Proctor's post.

I fail to understand why the post of Proctor has been made remunerative. Being a teacher, I consider it my primary duty to help the administration in improving discipline on the campus. For the discharge of my primary duty, I do not need any additional incentive. The proctorial assignment is causing embarrassment to me. I, therefore, find myself unable to accept the same.

On my own behalf and on the behalf of the Teachers' Association, I assure you full co-operation in matters relating to the improvement of academic atmosphere on the campus.

With regards,

Yours faithfully,
Arun Kumar Sinha
(A K Sinha)
Lecturer in English, L S College
&
General Secretary, University Depts & L S College
Teachers' Association, Muzaffarpur

Copy to:
Principal,
L S College, Muz

A Gandhian Thinker and Practitioner

Prof. Sinha was a 'Gandhian activist, thinker and believer in the Gandhian doctrine for social reconstruction.'[15] For Prof. Sinha, 'Gandhiji's non-violence asks us not to seek a special destiny for ourselves- a destiny apart from and above that of the people toiling in the fields and factories.'[16] In fact, Gandhian vision was one which had the potential to bring about social equality and peace, if understood and applied in true spirit.

> Violence is born from inequality. A society which pays disproportionate value to wealth is bound to be based on violence, suppression, oppression, corruption, militarism…Non-violence as exemplified by Gandhiji's abiding faith in the value of Charkha is a moral, spiritual, political and above all economic power. But the self has to be mastered. The non-violent man has to be a fighter for truth, a Satyagrahi. [17]

Belief in Hemingway's Mantra: "Courage Is Grace Under Pressure"

It is rather ironical that while he chose long cuts in life, life chose longer cuts for him. While some severe, life-changing and deeply disturbing family problems slowed him down, he still somehow grappled with his dilemma of remaining faithful to his teaching profession vis-à-vis his socio-political work. It was a dilemma worth the comparison with the ones faced by Shakesperean tragic characters—how to be true to one's basic responsibilities of being a teacher while being part of issues that also impacted the academic environments. Somehow he found a balance whereas the teacher of English literature was not supposed to be immersed in his literary texts only oblivious of his socio-political and economic environs, but he was also called upon to engage himself with social issues. And this he followed in concrete terms.

And though his personality embodied the both worlds, it did cause untold suffering and struggle to him as a human being. Behind the flourish of language, depth of understanding and empathy with social causes that came to us as a well-made 'product'—he fancied his lectures in the literature class rooms as a kind of performance where the teacher had to act out his interpretations in loud, lucid and lingering voice in order to reach out to the students who came from various socio-economic backgrounds and had differing levels of understanding—there were many disturbing personal and domestic factors that were all kept under painful control. No wonder, Hemingway's'courage is grace under pressure' were his most quoted words.

Donation of Books to Motipur College: When the Motipur College of Muzaffarpur district was to be granted the status of a constituent college of Bihar University by UGC, its governing body of the college through Prof. Abhay Kumar Shrivastava of its Chemistry department (who was also Prof. Sinha's next door neighbour at the time in around 1980 at Ramani Mohan Garden, Kalam Bagh Road, Muzaffarpur), asked for some books for their college library. Without blinking an eye-lid, Prof. Sinha donated more than 200 books from his personal collection. Such a gesture was rather unusual, because all the books were bought out of his personal hard earned money. The College sent him a message that his name would be displayed in the college library as one of the donators of books to the library. One does not know, however, if Prof. Sinha ever bothered to find out if the college kept its promise—for him the fact that books would be made available to the students studying in the interior part of North Bihar was a big satisfaction in itself.

Interestingly, Prof. Abhay Kumar Shrivastava, who later moved to join L S College, became Bursar, when Prof. Sinha became the Principal of the College. Later Prof. Shrivastava himself rose to become the Principal of the college.

His writings

A sample of his writing may be illustrative to make out the simplicity and lucidity of his language and the ability to communicate complex and serious text even to the lay reader. The opening paras of his work on Eliot under the introductory chapter 'Life and Literary Background' is worth reproducing:

> Who cares for poetry in the 2000s? This question arises in the mind of even those who care for poetry, because caring for poetry or any other art form cannot stand on its own. Life has always been a tangled web, and yet men and women have never given up caring for life. It is a truism but worth recalling that a true work of art helps us–and each work does it in its own way–in disintegrating the essential from the inessential, and makes life and living less bewildering and more meaningful.
>
> There are certain creative writers–their number is small–to whom we turn again and again for renewal of our faith in those values that give meaning and substance to the otherwise dull business of living. Dante and Shakespeare from the Western world may be placed in this category. And more than any other poet-critic of our times, Eliot has nearly 'fought' to make the contemporary educated public interested in the reading and appreciation of poetry. It is reassuring to hear from him that poetry will most likely continue to matter in all times:
>
> 'There is not one of us who is born with, or who suddenly acquires at puberty or later, an infallible discrimination and taste. The person

whose experience is limited is always liable to be taken in by the sham or the adulterate article, and we see generation after generation of untrained readers being taken in by the sham and adulterate in own time–indeed preferring them, for they are more easily assimilable than the genuine article. Yet, a large number of people, I believe, have the native capacity for enjoying some good poetry…' (The Use of Poetry and the Use of Criticism, 1933)[18]

One more sample from his unpublished novel in English may also be relevant to reproduce for the readers. These are actually opening lines of the novel, which is loosely autobiographical, so to say:

The fascination for the big, long word, more for the word itself than for what it means or suggests—this is almost a sensual fascination. 'Almost' because we shy away from such a thing as word—fascination. And words don't die. Memories of places, those we loved and are no more, fade away for ever, but words walk out of the cold storage, as it were, and surprise us like forgotten acquaintances. They sometimes come to stay. Per-so-na-li-ty…how did Ram Bahadur negotiate the tentative beginning, the soft and stable rise, the silken yet steady fall of the five-syllable word? The poor weaver might have winced as the father drooled. Despite his some English, Ram Bahadur couldn't catch the sense of the time. It was time to dare more and drool less. It was time to cut down on words, on personalities. Shiva won't wait for the cloud caused by Veer's illness to disperse. From books of history he had learnt that the contradictions can't be wished away. The conclusion is never reached; one only moved towards it, uncertainly yet doggedly. Moreover, Shiva was always short of patience. He'd start a thing and then wonder what to do next. So he brushed aside father's advice to wait and had the old building—except for the older northern portion—razed to the ground. The entire family was made to seek shelter in the sensibly unrazed portion which comprised one very large room (here trunks served for beds) and dung-smelling shed, where the cows (they were never more than two in number) were hustled into in rains and cold. During the two month long summer vacations, Shiva read and mused over Shakespeare and Milton in this dungish but cool corner.

Nothing exhilarates more than the sight of a habitation coming up. It has the touch of a new civilization taking shape. It didn't matter if the architect was called from a big city or the village mason made the design or it emerged from the stubborn resolve of Shiva or from the unarticulated blessing of his parents. What mattered was that it was coming up. Shiva had started with a shaky fund and on assurance from Iqbal that he'd not let shortage of material stand in the way. Iqbal became the backbone, and it was later found that his advice should have been better avoided. Why were the bricks which were extricated from the rubble of the razed portion used in the foundation of the new house? Ram Bahadur's sullen silence was not warranted. Didn't he see that Shiva had neither time nor experience to take care of the sundry details? Shiva's mother fumed and fretted but couldn't succeed in breaking the strong indifference of her husband. Perhaps the discomfiture he suffered over Rukmini's marriage had weakened the parental chord for ever.

Ram Bahadur's unnatural indifference was, however, swept away by the rising current of jealousy, intra-caste rivalries, deliberate villainy and much more, which constituted the essential diet of life in the village called Satnampur. Shiva was still a stranger to the unimaginably endless drama behind the still life of the village which was, by any means, large and ever expanding in terms of population. There was not much wealth, and almost no striving after it, hardly a thing called aspiration could be spotted, but its very size, its proximity to the district town & therefore to the law courts, besides a sizeable Muslim population which was in terms of consciousness more vibrant—all these and more made Satnampur in the early 1950s a spark waiting to ignite.

Shiva knew about the topography and demography of his village but as remotely as he knew the places on the maps of India and England.

So when Iqbal was heckled by a group of youths for absolutely no provocation from the former, Shiva was more than surprised. He was still in his early twenties and he had travelled remarkably far in life because of hard work and, of course, a modicum of opportunity. He didn't ever think that he had grown into a sort of nucleus around him unfamiliar sensations would arise and clash for prominence. Iqbal was hated because he had occupied the whole space where Shiva stood and moved in the stupefied imagination of the people in the village. It was more than a pressure on the emotion; the equation of power in the village looked like shifting from the southern tip to the western, where the new house was coming up.

You live in relation to others, howsoever aloof, secluded, taciturn you may be. They will catch you by the scruff of your neck. They will catch you and bring you to the ground, maim you for life if you don't acknowledge their presence and their limitless tine for surveillance. Shiva's intelligence, his insight were put on test by the assault on Iqbal which the latter had, smartly, shrugged off. Shiva could see that the incident might trigger off a Hindu-Muslim row, besides the scare of the police raid on the village upset his nerves. Finding himself so close to the cause of the possible flare-up, Shiva rushed to his father. That broke Ram Bahadur's indifference.[19]

Multiple influences and diverse interests

If one has to just name a few writers and thinkers who shaped his persona, his world view and whom he kept reading and also kept teaching about, it should be something like this: Buddha, Gandhi, Marx, Lenin, Vivekananda, Ambedkar, Nehru (with reservations), M N Roy, Acharya Narendra Dev, Lohia, JP, Vinoba Bhave, Donne, Shakespeare, Byron, Keats, Hardy, Browning, Wilde, Eliot, Lawrence, Hemingway, Tolstoy, Dostoevsky, Yeats, Dylan Thomas, Premchand,

Jainendra Kumar, Muktibodh, Ajneya, Marquez, Neruda etc. However, it would be lopsided if his life-long admiration for the Hindi film star Dev Anand, in particular, and to the great entertaining and informative role played by Hindi cinema, in general, are missed out. Similarly his love for the Pete Samprases, Nadals, Federars, Maradonas, of the world needs to be mentioned in the similar vein which many a time kept him glued to television during ungodly hours—the same hours that he chose to say good night forever in his characteristic unassuming manner.

A reference to a write-up on his last days written by his son, which appeared under the heading 'The Strong, Brown God' in the 'Speaking Tree' Column of the Edit page of *The Times of India* may be in order to underline the sense of detachment with which Prof. Sinha lived life.[20]

Here, it may be apt to quote the following lines from great Hindi poet Ramdhari Singh Dinkar, which were translated by Prof. Sinha into English and at once become a tribute to his faith in the power of poetry, a life of action with detachment, while also holding a light to his accomplishments as a translator:

> Bari kavita ki jo is bhumi ko sunder banati hai,
> Bara vah gyan jisse vyarth ki chinta nahin hoti,
> Bara vah aadmi jo jindagi bhar kam karta hai,
> Bara vah ruh jo roye bina tan se nikal jati.
> (Great is the poetry that makes this earth beautiful,
> Great that knowledge which doesn't cause useless strain.
> Great the man who works all his life,
> Great is that soul which leaves the body without a tear.)[21]

Prof. Sinha himself wrote very few poems–some love poems and a political poem on the hanging of the Pakistani leader and former Prime Minister, Zulfikar Ali Bhutto (5 January 1928 – 4 April 1979) by the Military ruler General Zia-ul-Haque–which was widely seen as rather unjust end of a popular democratic leader.

This poem on Bhutto has, as far as we know, remained unpublished. It was written on 5th April 1979, the very next day of Bhutto's execution the previous day. It thus carries the powerful sentiment for the tragedy of the democratic leader among the intelligentsia and democratic activists in India and elsewhere. The poem was located in Prof. Sinha's personal diaries after his demise and was uploaded on his second death anniversary, 28th November 2013, on a website dedicated to him. It may be instructive to end this essay by reproducing that 8-line poem here:

A POEM FOR BHUTTO[22]

Remembering you after you are no more
Seems to be a sin
I can't help.
For I see my doom
Coming to take me from my bed—
Oh Lord, hold the sky,
It's toppling all over the place,
While my father eats off my flesh

Arun Kumar Sinha

Composed on 5th April, '79

CHAPTER 18

BHAIYA, MY BROTHER

From Ghalib to Ogden Nash, From Camus to Kishore Kumar, From Naseeruddin Shah to Mike Brayerly

The earliest image of my elder brother—for me, *bhaiya*, as I called him— that I remember is perhaps of 1977–78, when, I, as a four year old or so, sitting among the audience with my parents and elder sister, just could not understand why all the family members were going gaga about a King with a moustache and in royal robes speaking a strange language (English) with a strange tone acting on the stage. That was my brother, Shri Kumar Vivek (14th July 1967–30th April 1997), perhaps ten or eleven years old, in a school play being staged at Convent School, Kalambagh Chowk, Muzaffarpur, Bihar. It must have been some kind of an annual day or so, and I remember vividly that it was late in the evening, with faces of people sitting around enveloped in darkness. Today, when we complete 16 years of his passing away, I feel like sharing a few things about him.

A brilliant—almost gifted—student, I sometime really marvel at his multidimensional interests. He always stood first in his class and topped in matriculation examination in his school. The subjects that he opted for in his Intermediate Arts (IA) (Junior college or 11th-12th) at Langat Singh College, Muzaffarpur, were, besides the compulsory Hindi and English, Political Science, Economics, Sanskrit and Mathematics. In his IA exams, he got more marks in Mathematics than Political Science, thus Mathematics became his main subject, with Political Science being treated as an 'extra', even though he had obtained first division marks. It needs to be underlined that during those days in early 1980s, securing First Division was a great achievement obtained by only the meritorious ones as the rat race of securing 90%+ had yet to start. In B.A, he opted for Economics Honours with Mathematics and English Literature. At that time in 1984, they had just introduced a system of BA with 2years Passcourse+1year Hons. system, which meant that in the first two years, one had to study full-fledged papers in all three subjects, with last one year being dedicated to Honours course to be opted from these subjects. He opted for Economics Honours and secured perhaps the second highest marks in the University with 61% or so.

In the early 1980s, he had some rich and strange range of reading habits—he regularly subscribed to *Sarika*, the Hindi literary magazine brought out by TOI; to that film magazine with its tabloid shape and its name **g** written in big letters; that hip-hop magazine *Sun (*introducing us to names like Micheal Jackson, Elton John, George Michael)*;* the newly emerging area of interest of IT covered by that magazine called *Computer*. Among books, besides some of the bestsellers of Alistair Maclean, Arthur Hailey, Sideney Sheldon and "the ilk", one would often see him coming back from his evening strolls in the market with books produced by Rajkamal Paperbacks. I was six and five months younger to him, and my sister one and four months. First my sister, and later I, got introduced to an entire range of Hindi writers through him—Mohan Rakesh, Kamleshwar, Nirmal Verma, Mannu Bhandari, Dharamveer Bharati, Amarkant, Kamtanath, Krishna Sobti, Usha Priyamvada, among many others, and also Hindi translations of other language writers like those of Quratulain Haider, Amrita Pritam, to name just two. My bhaiya also had some kind of fascination for the satirists, and hence one got introduced to Harishankar Parsai, Rabindranath Tyagi, Shrilal Shukla, Sharad Joshi, Amrit Rai. No wonder, his diary entries, which are basically a collage of quotations taken from a wide range of writers and poets, one could also notice repeated quotes from none other than the great Contemporary American Poet–Satirist, Ogden Nash, with his poem on 'Octopus', being his favourite. His fine sense of humour certainly 'justified' this inclination, so to say.

Bhaiya did not know how to read or write Urdu script, but because of his special interest in Ghazals, he would buy Urdu poets' collections available in Devnagari—from Mir, Ghalib, Bahadur Shah Zafar, Iqbal, Firaq to Shaharyar, he built up a good collection of Urdu poetry. Basically, he himself wrote a few ghalzals, poems in Hindi, beside a few in English, and one could see him making reference to Urdu-Hindi dictionary in Devnagari to understand and make use of Urdu/Persian expressions. Among Hindi poets I remember the collections of Raghuvir Sahay, Sarveshwar Dayal Saxena, Srikant Verma, Nagarjun and Muktibodh. Most of these books, including the ones from Rajkamal Paperbacks, he would often borrow from a library called Suvidh Sangh, of which he was a member, located near Nitishwar Singh College of Muzaffarpur.

In fact, this search for peculiar Urdu expressions also reverberated in English, because I find that some of his diary quotes are about strange words in English. For example, much before I became a student of English literature and later had an opportunity to co-author a book on Eliot with my father, I read this word 'polyphiloprogenitive' written in his notebook with its meaning (literally to be fond of children or prolific, but in Eliot it has other meanings). This is the word with which Eliot's poem 'Mr. Eliot's Sunday Morning Service' begins. I think he was turning out to be that perfect blend of Indian and western culture, which my father had desired to be—sending him to Hindi medium schools and training him to change over to English medium in a very natural fashion after the 10th, a system which I also had to follow courtesy my brother doing it successfully and eminently.

Two more information are worth sharing: One was his love for some of the French writers like Sartre, Camus and poets like Baudelaire (this information I am adding after being reminded of it by my elder cousin Shri Nirmalanshu Ranjan). Secondly, his passionate love for cricket—an avid listener of cricket commentary, which he would also ape in mohalla cricket, he had prepared his own cricket photo album of his superstars like Imran Khan, Sunil Gavaskar, Viv Richards and John Michael Brearley (Mike Brearley) cutting their photos from newspapers and magazines. Among the magazines that he read regularly I should have also mentioned 'Sportstar' and 'Cricket Samrat'. This cricket photo album also had some of the important score sheets of various important matches that he had painstakingly prepared—remember these were pre-television times mostly. After his matriculation in 1982, he started a sort of badminton club with his neighbourhood friends, which really attracted a good number of 'spectators', because of the novelty of tournament type arrangement—professional nets, racquets, maintenance of score cards, refrees etc. After the coming of television, he did get hooked on to Tennis and cricket, watching them in the middle of nights or in the wee-hours, when the matches were relayed from the 'Down Under'.

In the neighbourhood cricket team, he was always chosen to captain the side by his friends, not really because of his cricketing skills, which were limited to slow medium bowling and better batting, but mainly because of his captaincy skills—for field placements, for change of bowling in a strategic manner and so on and so forth. No wonder, his one of the model cricketers was Mike Brayerly, the legendary captain of England in the 1970s, who was known to be a master-captain, and was kept in the side not as much because of his cricketing skills as such, but because of his 'captaincy skills.'

But my bhaiya had two problems: he was quite an introvert and over-sensitive. His bathroom singing of Kishore Kumar's songs, love for the parallel as well as masala action films including James Bonds'— he was a die-hard fan of both Amitabh Bachchan and Naseeruddin Shah—perhaps showed a zest and intensity and range for life which proved too much for the space and time he was placed in. This aspect of his personality with his ingrained desires to overcome the surroundings of Muzaffarpur, put him in direct conflict with my father's Gandhian idealism on the one hand, and, more importantly, with the rather apathetic social ambience of Bihar of the 1990s. From 1991 onwards, bhaiya developed acute psychological depression, with which he fought for nearly six intense and painflul years, ultimately succumbing to it in 1997—two and half months before he could turn even 30—ironically, as a 'drop-out' student of MA (Economics).

Needless to say, the overall deteriorating atmosphere on the campus of college and universities of Bihar starting in 1980s and taking on entirely new colours in the 1990s, added to his derailment, with academic sessions getting delayed by more than two years and examinations happening haphazardly, almost chaotically. I have always seen the deterioration of my bhaiya as somekind of concrete manifestation of social deterioration, though my father generally never shared my understanding because of his immense faith in social ethos, and always tried to analyse it as a personal failure—a reading which I thought was too cruel on himself and bhaiya.

His rather incomplete life reminds me of that incomplete play that he once decided to stage with his neighbourhood friends in which I had also got a minor role, perhaps of a girl. This might have been the summer of 1982—his post-matriculation examination and pre-results days— when bhaiya took out a play from the magazine for the young adults 'Paraag' that used to be brought out by *TOI* group. He edited it suitably, and cobbled together many of his friends—boys as well as girls—and proper rehearsals got started. My father asked a few of his students to help the team out in managing the show. However, after some days of rehearsals, which was really fun, everything just evaporated probably because a few of the parents were not very appreciative of the growing up boys and girls working together for a play.

Here I reproduce his poem in his own handwriting, which had appeared in 'Vaishali', the magazine of Langat Singh College, perhaps sometime in 1984–85 or may be earlier. An English translation of the Poem as attempted by me has also been appended after the original Hindi.

एक पृथ्वी अब भी घूम रही है

लोग मुझे बताते हैं ----
पृथ्वी अब भी घूम रही है
सूरज की रोशनी इससे छिनी नहीं है,
चाँद अपना आकार स्थिर नहीं कर पाया है.
फिर बदले लिबास में चीजें क्यों लगती
हैं मुझे?

शायद इसलिए कि
मेरे संबंध उन पलकों से टूट गए हैं
जिनके साथ कभी मेरा वजूद उठता-गिरता था
शायद इसलिए कि
मैं वह खुलूस नहीं महसूसता आज
जो तुम्हारी शख्सियत की हिद्दत होती थी,
और जिसके छूते जिन्दगी के रिसते
नासूरों पर
मैं ठंडक उलीच पाता था ---
या फिर इसलिए कि
अब वह मंजिल कहीं भी नहीं होती जान
पड़ती
जिसे हमने इस यकीन से दूर रख छोड़ा था,
कि आते सफर की दुश्वारियों का आतंक
हमारे जुड़ाव में नयी गाँठें डालता रहेगा,
लेकिन जिसके दूर-दूर रहने ने
हमारी चाही हुई एक गाँठ को मजबूत
नहीं बनाया
बल्कि जिससे पूरा संबंध सूत ही गाँठों में तब्दील
हो गया

लेकिन --- लेकिन इन सोचों के हथौड़ों
का प्रभुत्व
क्यों कर मुझ पर छाता जा रहा है?
क्या मैं नहीं जानता ---
चाँद अपना आकार स्थिर नहीं कर पाया है,
सूरज की रोशनी उससे छिनी नहीं है,
पृथ्वी अब भी घूम रही है ---

[ONE] The Earth is Still Rotating

People tell me
The earth is still rotating
The rays of the sun have not been snatched from it
The moon is yet to stabilise its shape
Yet why do I find things around me in changed gears?

May be because
My interactions with those eyelids are now broken
With whose fall and lift my very existence was aligned
Perhaps because I no longer feel the warmth
Which the intensity of your persona transmitted
Acting as a balm
On the oozing sores of my life
Or may be that destination no longer seems possible
Which we had kept a bit far away
Believing that the trials of the upcoming journey
Would keep adding new knots
But our distant existence
Did not strengthen the knots that we had desired to achieve
Rather the entire relationship turned into a web of knots

But...but... why are these strong hammering thoughts
Completely overpowering me
Don't I realise…
The moon is yet to stabilise its shape
The rays of the sun have not been snatched from it
And the earth is still rotating

Kumar Vivek

CHAPTER 19

MALE BONDING

An Autobiographical Essay in Verse

My mother, my wife, my daughter
My sister in the background—
Their sweet, feminine voices
Their typical dresses—saris, salwars, feminine shirts-pants, frocks

Now only the other species surround me in our house.
My brother, his deep voice gone for ever
Wearing a full sleeved rolled shirt, pair of trousers
and donning a moustache, walked briskly into the recesses of time.

Father, hung his boots at the onset of the last winters
Without a warning, unlike his loud and clear voice
Cloaked in pyjama and kurta, or in trousers and shirts
That woke up us siblings in the mornings for schools like daily rituals.

Lesser number of stallion pair of shoes in the house
Shaving cream of only one variety, single brush
And a razor to boot, virile underpants of single size
Soak on the balcony, reminding me of the ones that were bought for me

For the first time by father and brother
Years back (accosting me secretly into the bedroom
That summer evening, smiling as well as concerned
To check if they fitted me—myself all too embarrassed and proud and confused.)

A man-grove of males gone forever
I stand singled out in the altered sex-ratio
With my odd voice, machogears, and appetite
Like a grown-up sapling among the heap of fallen trees sticking its neck out—

My gynic life-givers protecting me heroically
Taking me for some endangered species.

[Published in the journal *Indian Literature* brought out by Sahitya Akademi, India, issue no. 271 (September/October 2012)]

NOTES AND REFERENCES

Introduction

1. The statue has been there since 1861 itself and was put up parallelly to the statue of another 'famous' British general, Charles Napier, who played a significant role in seizing Sindh for the British in 1853
2. https://www.findagrave.com/memorial/80431412/henry-havelock #source
3. https://www.theguardian.com/uk/2000/oct/20/london.politicalnews
4. https://www.dailymail.co.uk/news/article-9142391/Row-erupts-decision-rename-road-honoured-British-general-founder-Sikhism.html
5. Buckland, C. E. 'Entry on Neill, James George Smith', *Dictionary of Indian Biography*. Swan Sonnenschein, London, 1906, p. 314 (https://archive.org/details/dictionaryofindi00buckuoft/page/314/mode/1up?view=theater)
6. Kaye, John William. *A History of the Sepoy War in India 1857-1858*, London; New York; Bombay; Longmans, Green, and Co., 1896.
7. Nayar, Pramod K. *The Penguin 1857 Reader*, Penguin India, New Delhi, 2007, p. 144

8. Ibid, p.13
9. *Young India*, 29-9-1927 included in *The Collected Works of Mahatma Gandhi*, Vol. 40, p. 178 (https://www.gandhiashramsevagram.org/gandhi-literature/mahatma-gandhi-collected-works-volume-40.pdf)
10. https://web.archive.org/web/20120812032435/http://pd.cpim.org/2007/0415/04152007_1857.htm
11. *Young India*, 13-10-1927 included in *The Collected Works of Mahatma Gandhi*, Vol. 40, p. 250 (https://www.gandhiashramsevagram.org/gandhi-literature/mahatma-gandhi-collected-works-volume-40.pdf)
12. https://web.archive.org/web/20120812032435/http://pd.cpim.org/2007/0415/04152007_1857.htm
13. https://www.change.org/p/south-ayrshire-council-remove-the-statue-of-james-george-smith-neill-from-wellington-square-in-ayr
14. https://francescobonfanti88.medium.com/the-butcher-of-allahabad-ce23da5fc7e5
15. https://thewire.in/world/statues-racism-history-protests (published on 27.06.2020)
16. Memmi, Albert. *Decolonization and the Decolonized*, (Translated from the French by Robert Bononno), University of Minnesota Press, Minneapolis, 2006, p. xii
17. Ibid, p. 14
18. Berger, John. *Ways of Seeing*, Penguin Books, UK, 1990
19. Nicolas, Jack. *Men's Liberation: A New Definition of Masculinity*, Penguin Books; Open market, New York, 1975
20. Piercy, Marge. *Women on the Edge of Time*, Alfred A. Knoff, New York, 1976, p. 357

Chapter 1

1. https://www.thelancet.com/journals/langlo/article/PIIS2214-109X(21)00094-2/fulltext

2. "Where have Kerala's 'missing' girl children gone?" http://articles.timesofindia.indiatimes.com/2012-03-19/thiruvananthapuram/31209985_1_female-foeticide-girl-child-ratio
3. "Adverse Juvenile Sex Ratio in Kerala". *http://www.epw.in/commentary/adverse-juvenile-sex-ratio-kerala.html*
4. Chapman, Wes. "Why I Am (Not) a Feminist." http://sun.iwu.edu/~wchapman/whyfem.html
5. 'The Education of Boys: A Submission to Standing Committee on Employment, Education and Workplace Relations', from the South Australian Association of State School Organisations Inc to House of Representatives, Australia, www.aphref.aph.gov. au_house_committee_edt_eofb_subs_sub55.pdf (Full text of Steve Biddulph's article can be accessed at www.manhood.com.au)
6. Steinem, Gloria. Documents from the "Women's Liberation Movement: An On-line Archival Collection." Special Collections Library, Duke University.
7. Namishray, Mohandas. *Apne Apne Pinjare*. Vaani Prakashan 1996. (Translation of the cited extract by Kumar Vikram)
8. Originally published in *No More Fun and Games: A Journal of Female Liberation*, Cambridge, Mass: Cell No 16, Vol.1, no. 2 (Feb 1969)
9. Weathers, Mary Ann. "Women's Liberation Movement: An On-line Archival Collection." Special Collections Library, Duke University', https://repository.duke.edu/dc/wlmpc

Chapter 2

1. Hansen, Kathryn, (Eds.) Alice Thorner and Maithreyi Krishnaraj. 'The *Virangana* in North Indian History: Myth and Popular Culture'. *Ideals, Images and Real Lives: Women in Literature and History*, (Eds.) Alice Thorner and Maithreyi Krishnaraj. Orient Longman (for Sameeksha Trust), Mumbai, 2000, p. 257
2. Beale, Thomas William, (Ed.) Henry George Keene. *An Oriental Biographical Dictionary*, I[st] Indian Ed., 1972, Kalyani Press, Ludhiana.

3. Ibid, p.309
4. In this context, it is worthwhile to refer to the differing perceptions about Shahjahan's two daughters Jahanara and Roshanara. The former has been viewed quite sympathetically for being a caring daughter who nursed her father quite religiously in his last days. However, Roshanara bears the brunt for being a bad daughter as she sided with her brother Aurangzeb. The difference in the perception is perhaps due to the fact that Jahanara did not rebel against the male authority as symbolized by her father whereas Roshanara committed the crime of rebellion. This despite the fact that rebellion on the part of the son against the father was the order of the day as seen in the cases of the unsuccessful ones by Jahangir and Shahjahan against their fathers and successful one by Aurangzeb. However, whereas these rebellions of the sons are viewed and explained in terms of medieval or Timurid traditions, in the context of Roshanara, it becomes the personal characteristic of a daughter who failed to stand by her father.
5. A full treatment of the way proverbs around the world about women share the general androcentric perception about the 'subordinate' status of women can be seen in the book titled after the above-referred proverb. This Dutch original title available in English translation is an outcome of the study by Mineke Schipper, published in English translation by Yale University Press, New Haven and London, 2004. The publicity folder of the book brought out by the publisher Foundation for the Production and Translation of Dutch Literature has an interesting observation to make. It says, *"Striking similarities emerge across cultures. Mothers, for example, are praised around the world: 'Mother is God number two' (Malawi) and 'Mother's milk is holy' (Mongolian), whereas wives seem to be a problem: 'Never marry a woman with bigger feet than your own' is advice from Mozambique, but amazingly a Chinese saying contains exactly the same message, and even uses the same metaphor. Those big feet refer to female talents, and all over the world proverbs seem to warn against marrying women with*

more talents or education than they have themselves." Read along side this observation, Kathryn Hansen's comments in the above-cited essay on 'Virangana', about the Hindu tradition of goddesses symbolising *Shakti,* enlarges our understanding of this complex issue all the more. She states (p.259): "*Hindu mythology offers another important female paradigm which contrasts with the wifely ideal, namely, the mother goddess. The goddess, whether manifest in her benign aspect as Lakshmi or Paravati, or in her more menacing form as Kali or Durga, derives her power fundamentally from her relationship as mother rather than as spouse, a role in which she exercises distinctive female control through the ability to generate and nurture life.*"

6. Saxena, Neela Bhattacharya. "Desire To Be", *In the Beginning is Desire: Tracing Kali's Footprints in Indian Literature,* Indialog Publications Pvt Ltd, New Delhi, 2004 (especially in the chapter on Ismat Chugtai's *The Crooked Line* titled 'Desire To Be', p. 174-207)
7. That Haji Begam accompanied Humayun in his Persian exile and made this tomb for her husband has been referred to by the French critic Alexander Papadopoulo in his book *Islam and Muslim Art* translated from the French by Robert Erich Wolf, Henry N. Abrams Inc. Publishers, New York, 1979, p. 288.
8. Asher, Catherine B. *Architecture of Mughal India (The New Cambridge History of India)*, Cambridge University Press, New Delhi, 1992, p. 44
9. Mannering, Douglas. *Great Works of Indian Art,* Smithmarks Books, New York, 1996, p. 35
10. (Quoted by) Krishnaswamy N. *Contemporary Literary Theory: A Student's Companion.* Macmillan, New Delhi, 2001, p. 75

Chapter 4

1. Prasad, Rajendra. *Autobiography.* Penguin Books India, 2010, New Delhi, p.46-47
2. Sinha, Sachchidanand. "Mahesh Narayan", *Some Eminent Behar Contemporaries.* Janaki Prakashan, Patna, 1946, p. 42-43

3. Roy, Ramashray. "Caste and Political Recruitment in Bihar", *Caste in Indian Politics.* (Ed.) Rajani Kothari, Orient Blackswan, New Delhi, 1995, p. 225
4. Pandey, Shreedhar Narayan. *Education and Social Changes in Bihar 1900-1921: A Survey of Social History of Bihar from Lord Curzon to Non- Cooperation Movement,* Motilal Banarasi Dass, Varanasi, 1975, p. 196
5. Prasad, Rajendra. *Autobiography*, Penguin Books India, 2010, New Delhi, p.46-47
6. Desai, A R. *Social Background of Indian Nationalism.* Popular Prakashan, Bombay, First Pub. 1948, Fifth Edition 1976, Reprint 1982, p. 153
7. Ibid., pp.153-154
8. Chandra, Bipan. *Modern India.* National Council of Educational Research and Training, New Delhi, First Pub. 1971, Reprint 1986, pp. 119-120

Chapter 5

1. Hasan, Mushirul. "The Great Akbar of Independence Struggle". *The Hindu.* http://www.thehindu.com/opinion/lead/the-great-akbar-of-independence struggle/article5326492.ece
2. Qaiser, Rizwan. *Resisting Colonialism and Communal Politics: Maulana Azad and the Making of the Indian Nation.* Manohar Publishers and Distributors, New Delhi, 2011.
3. http://articles.timesofindia.indiatimes.com/2011-09-09/edit-page/30130923_1_muslims-pakistan-communities
4. http://www.columbia.edu/itc/mealac/pritchett/00litlinks/txt_azad_congress_1940.html
(The full speech is also included in 'Document 51', *The Selected Works of Maulana Abul Kalam Azad,* (Vol. 1, 1936-42) Chief Editor Ravindra Kumar, Atlantic Publishers & Distributors, New Delhi, 1991, pp. 96-114

Chapter 6

1. Moeran, Brian. *Creativity at Work: An Anthropological Analysis of Book Fairs.* September 2008. http://www.scribd.com/doc/93752020/Bookfair-Analysis
2. Fuller Danielle. "Up Close and Personal: Why Readers love 'live' book events". Conference on Book Cultures, Book Events: The Transnational Culture, Commerce and Social Impact of Literary Festivals, University of Stirling, 23–24 March 2012. http://www.bookcultures.stir.ac.uk
3. Horne, Alastair. "The Future's Live, the Future's Digital: Why Publishers Should Embrace Live Events in a Digital Age". http://www.bookcultures.stir.ac.uk
4. Nawotka, Edward. 'In China and the UAE Book Fairs Civilize Business-Minded Metropolises", *Publishing Perspectives,* March 8 2011, (http://publishingperspectives.com/2011/03/china-uae-book-fairs-civilize-business-minded-metropolises/

Chapter 7

1. *National Youth Readership Survey* was conducted by National Book Trust, India through National Council of Applied Economic Research between 2009–2010. Report was published in book form: Shukla, Rajesh. *Indian Youth: Demographics and Readership: Results from the National Youth Readership Survey,* National Book Trust, India and National Council of Applied Economic Research, New Delhi, 2010
2. Text of Barack Obama's Speech Courtesy: http://www.asksam.com/ebooks/releases.asp?file=ObamaSpeeches.ask&dn=American%20Library%20Association

Chapter 8

1. Desai, A.R. *Social Background of Indian Nationalism,* Popular Prakashan, First Edition 1948, Reprint 1982, Bombay, p. 1

2. Edward Hallett "Ted" Carr (28 June 1892 – 3 November 1982) was a liberal realist and later left-wing Marxist British historian, journalist and international relations theorist. Carr was best known for his 14-volume history of the Soviet Union, in which he provided an account of Soviet history from 1917 to 1929, for his writings on international relations, and for his book *What Is History?*
3. Heywood, Andrew. *Political Theory: An Introduction (Second ed)*, London: Macmillan Press, 1999 pp. 97–98
4. Kashyap, Subhash C. *Our Political System*, National Book Trust, India, First Edition 2008, Reprinted 2010, New Delhi, p. 9
5. Here Aloysius writes in a footnote: For instance, wars between groups in pre-modern times were largely known as wars between ethnic or racial groups.
6. Aloysius, G. *Nationalism Without a Nation in India*, Oxford University Press, 1997, New Delhi, pp. 14-15
7. Hazen, Charles Downer (with additional 10 chapters by V D Mahajan). *Modern Europe (1789 Onwards)*, Published in India by S. Chand & Company by arrangement with M/s Henry Holt & Co., New York, First Published in India, 1956, Sixth Edition, 1987, New Delhi, p. 42
8. ibid, p. 295
9. Chaube, Shibani Kinkar. *The Making and Working of the Indian Constitution*, National Book Trust, India, 2009, New Delhi, p.4
10. Legouis, Emile, et al. *History of English Literature*, (Translated from the French by Helen Douglas Irvine), Macmillan India Limited, First Indian Edition 1981, Madras, pp. 591-92
11. Daiches, David. *A Critical History of English Literature (Vol. III)*, In Four Volumes, Allied Publishers Private Limited, First Indian Reprint 1979, New Delhi, (First Published by Martin & Warburg Ltd, London, 1960), pp. 556-57
12. ibid, p.556-57
13. Ibid, p. 557

14. Jr. William K Wimsatt and Cleanth Brookes. *Literary Criticism: A Short History*, Oxford & IBH Publishing Co. Pvt. Ltd., New Delhi (First published by Alfred A. Knopf. Inc., 1957), p. 183
15. *https://archive.org/stream/anessayofdramati00dryduoft/anessayofdramati00dryduoft_djvu.txt*
16. Jr. William K Wimsatt and Cleanth Brookes: *Op.cit*, p. 187
17. https://chaucer.fas.harvard.edu/preface-fables
18. Daiches: op. cit, pp. 574-75
19. Baker, Mona and Gabriela Saldanha (Ed.), *Routledge Encyclopedia of Translation Studies (2nd Edition)*, Routledge, New York, 1998, p. 35-36
20. Legouis and Cazamian: op. cit, p. 592
21. Eliot, T.S. *The Use of Poetry and the Use of Criticism: Studies in the Relation of Criticism to Poetry in England* (Charles Eliot Norton Lectures for 1932-33), 'Introduction', Harvard University Press, pp. 14-15
22. This concept of father-figure linked with the idea of nationalism has come in for sharp criticism in recent times from the feminists and the post-colonial critics. In a fine essay titled *Gender Essentialisms, Politicalisation and Peace Activism in the Region of the Former Yugoslavia*, Darija ŽiliÊ analyses nationalism and the concept of father-figure (http://www.nenasilje.org/publikacije/pdf/20poticaja/20pieces-zilic.pdf; accessed on 22.04.2011)

Chapter 9

1. Chandra, Bipan. *Modern India*, National Council of Educational Research and Training, First Published 1971, Reprint Edn. 1986, New Delhi, p. 51
2. "History of India: The British East India Company and Colonization", *From Trade to Colonization - Historic Dynamics of the East India Companies*, http://india_resource.tripod.com/eastindia.html (accessed on 17.04.2011)
3. Chandra, Bipan: op. cit, p. 37
4. Chandra, Bipan: op. cit, p. 149

5. Desai, A. R. *Social Background of Indian Nationalism*, Popular Prakashan, First Edition 1948, Reprint 1982, Bombay, pp. 387-388
6. Haldar, Gopal. *Languages of India* (Translated into English from the Original Bangla by Tista Bagchi), National Book Trust, India, 2000, New Delhi, pp. 184-186
7. President Chandrika Bandaranaike Kumaratunga delivered the First Madhavrao Scindia Memorial Lecture at the Taj Palace Hotel in New Delhi on April 23, 2002, Courtesy *Frontline*, Volume 19 - Issue 10, May 11-24, 2002
8. Haldar: *op. cit, p. 186*
9. Aloysius, G. *Nationalism Without a Nation in India*, Oxford University Press, 1997, New Delhi, pp. 14-15
10. Kesavan, B.S. *History of Printing and Publishing in India: A Story of Cultural Awakening (Vol. 1)*, National Book Trust, India, First Edition 1985, New Delhi, p. 3
11. ibid, p. 28 12. ibid, p. 37-38
13. ibid, p. 46
14. ibid, p. 42
15. ibid, pp. 60-61
16. ibid, p. 46
17. Wintermitz, Maurice. *History of Indian Literature (Vol. I)*, first published 1904, (A new authoritative translation from original German by V. Srinivasa Sarma), Motilal Banarsidas, 1981, Delhi, 'Introduction', p. 7
18. Chandra: op. cit, p. 91
19. Cohn, Bernard S. '*The Command of Language and the Language of Command', Subaltern Studies IV: Writings on South Asian History and Society (ed.) Ranajit Guha*, Oxford University Press, New Delhi, 1985, p. 288
20. Spear, Percival. *Oxford History of India*, Oxford University Press, 1958, New Delhi, p. 513
21. Wintermitz: op. cit, p. 9

22. Kesavan: op. cit, p. 253 23. ibid, pp. 395-404
24. Wintermitz: op. cit, p. 10
25. Kesavan: op. cit, p. 414
26. Quoted by Kesavan: ibid
27. Wintermitz: op. cit, p. 10
28. ibid.
29. Sankhdher, B.M. *India and the World Literature, British Poetical Literature on India 1780-1835*, Indian Council for Cultural Relations, 1990, New Delhi, p. 422
30. Cohn, Bernard S: Op. cit, p. 292
31. Wintermitz: op. cit, p. 10
32. Wintermitz: op. cit, p. 13-14
33. Chatterjee, Partha, *'Gandhi and the Critique of Civil Society', Subaltern Studies III: Writings on South Asian History and Society (ed.) Ranajit Guha,* Oxford University Press, New Delhi, 1985, p. 155
34. Das, Sisir Kumar. *Indian Ode to the West Wind,* 'Goethe and India: Towards a World Literature', Pencraft International, New Delhi, 2001, p. 120
35. Quoted by Kesavan, op. cit, p. 393 (from Das, Sisir Kumar. *Sahibs and Munshis,* 'Preface', Orion Publications, New Delhi, 1978
36. ibid.
37. Quoted by Partha Chatterjee: op. cit, p. 154
38. Das, Sisir Kumar. *Indian Ode to the West Wind,* 'India, Halhed and the Early British Orientalism', Pencraft International, New Delhi, 2001, p. 33
39. Sadiq, Muhammad. *A History of Urdu Literature,* Oxford University Press, Delhi, 1984, p. 291
40. Sadani, Jaikishandas. *India and the World Literature,* 'Indian Images in English Poetry', Indian Council for Cultural Relations, 1990, New Delhi, p. 447
41. Wintermitz: op. cit, p. 17
42. Chandra: op. cit, p. 124-125

43. Wintermitz: op. cit, p. 17
44. Chandra: op. cit, p. 120
45. http://www.columbia.edu/itc/mealac/pritchett/00generallinks/macaulay/txt_minute_education_1835.html (accessed on 24.04.2011)
46. Das, Sisir Kumar. *A History of Indian Literature (Vol. VIII): 1800-1910 Western Impact: Indian Response,* 'The Old Order: Stability and Change', Sahitya Akademi, 1991, New Delhi, p. 87
47. Cohn, Bernard S: Op. cit, p. 278
48. Das, Sisir Kumar. *A History of Indian Literature (Vol. VIII),* Op. cit. p. 42
49. Chandra: op. cit, p. 122
50. Quoted by Das: *A History of Indian Literature (Vol. VIII)*, op. cit, p. 256
51. Kunhappa Murkot. *Sree Narayan Guru*, National Book Trust, India, 1982, New Delhi, pp. 72-73
52. Prakritisation in the context of de-Persianisation and de-Sanskritisation has been suggested by Sisir Kumar Das, among others.
53. Das, Sisir Kumar. *Indian Ode to the West Wind, 'Shakespeare's Translations in Indian Languages'*, op. cit, p. 69
54. ibid, p. 63-64
55. Quoted by Sisir Kumar Das, ibid, p. 66
56. Mugali, R S. *History of Kannada Literature*, Sahitya Akademi, Delhi, 1975, p. 100
57. Satchidanandan, K. 'The Case of a Wounded Literature', *The Hindu*, 06.07.1997,http://www.cscsarchive.org:8081/MediaArchive/clippings.nsf/(docid)/609AD65599A3B9286 5256942003139E4, Accessed on 24.04.2011)
58. Quoted by Sisir Kumar Das: *Indian Ode to the West Wind*, 'Meghnad Badh Kavya': Indian Epic, Western Model', op. cit, p.114
59. Das, Sisir Kumar. *A History of Indian Literature (Vol. IX), 1911- 1956: Struggle for Freedom: Triumph and Tragedy*, Sahitya Akademi, 1995, New Delhi, p. 229
60. Das, Sisir Kumar. *A History of Indian Literature (Vol. IX):*, Op. cit, p. 258

61. Nair, P.K Parameswaran. *History of Malayalam Literature,* (translated from Malayalam by E. M. J. Venniyoor), Sahitya Akademi, 1967, New Delhi, p. 117-18
62. Chandra: op. cit, p. 119
63. Rice, Edward P. *A History of Kannada Literature, (Second Ed. Rev & Enlarged),* Asian Educational Services, New Delhi, 1982 (First Published 1921), pp.100-101
64. Das, Sisir Kumar.*A History of Indian Literature (Vol. VIII),* op. cit. 230
65. Zahar, Renate. *Frantz Fanon: Colonialism and Alienation, 'Man's Alienation in Colonialism',* (Translated by Willfried F. Feuser), Aakar Books (Published in agreement with Monthly Review Press, New York), First published in 1974, First published in India 2010), Delhi, p. 44
66. Verma, Nirmal. 'India and Europe', Yatra: One: Writings from the Indian Sub-Continent, General Editor: Alok Bhalla. (Eds.) Nirmal Verma and U R Ananthamurthy, An Imprint of HarperCollins Pvt. Ltd, New Delhi, 1993, p. 65

Chapter 10

1. Said, Edward. *Reflections on Exile and Other Literary and Cultural Essays,* Penguin Books, New Delhi, 2001
2. Said, Edward: Op. cit, p. 617
3. Said, Edward: Op. cit, p. Xxviii
4. Said, Edward: Op. cit, p. Xxxi
5. Dangle, Arjun. "Dalit Literature: Past, Present and Future", *Poisoned Bread: Translations from Modern Marathi Dalit Literature.,* Orient Longman, Hyderabad, 1992, p. 242
6. Said, Edward: Op. cit, p. Xxvii
7. Said, Edward: Op. cit, p. xxiii
8. Dangle, Arjun: op. cit, p. 289
9. *Hans,* August, 2004, p. 7

10. Said, Edward: Op. cit, p. Xxix
11. Said, Edward: Op. cit, p. Xxvii
12. Said, Edward: Op. cit, p. 384
13. Anand, S. "Affirmative Fictions", www.aiccindia.org, the website of The All India Christian Council
14. Dangle, Arjun. *Op. cit*, p. 303

Chapter 11

1. Senghor, Leopald Sedar. *Poems of a Black Orpheus.* Translated by William Oxley, The Menard Press (1 June 1981), London, ISBN 0903400596
2. *Time (magazine).* 17 November 1967. www.oxfordreference.com
3. *Reflections on Exile and Other Literary and Cultural Essays,* Edward W. Said, Penguin Books India 2001, p. xxvii
4. Soyinka, Wole. 'Religion and Human Rights'. https://journals.sagepub.com/doi/pdf/10.1080/03064228808534439
5. Mazuri, Ali A. "Wole Soyinka as a Television Critic: A Parable of Deception". *Transition*' No. 54 (1991). Published By: Indiana University Press, pp. 165-177, https://www.jstor.org/stable/2934911
6. Azad, Abul Kalam. Presidential Address to the Fifty-Third Session of the Indian National Congress, Ramgarh, 1940, http://www.columbia.edu/itc/mealac/pritchett/00litlinks/txt_azad_congress_1940.html
7. https://www.worldcat.org/title/chants-dombre/oclc/610616672

Chapter 12

1. http://www.columbia.edu/itc/mealac/pritchett/00urdu/kafan/taraqqi_1936_speech/txt_hindi.pdf (English translation of the quoted passage is by Kumar Vikram)
2. 'Toward an Impure Poetry' by Pablo Neruda. *Penguin,* Penguin Random House India, https://penguin.co.in/toward-an-impure-poetry-by-pablo-neruda/

Chapter 13

1. http://aboutreading.blogspot.com/2013/10/the-kalevipoeg-is-more-akin-to-our.html

Chapter 15

1. Moraes, Dom. *My Son's Father.* Penguin India, New Delhi, 1991

Chapter 16

1. Prof. Arun Kumar Sinha (1940–2011),who retired in August 2000 as Professor in English and Principal, Langat Singh College, B R A Bihar University, Muzaffarpur, Bihar.
2. Shri Sachidanand Sinha (1938-2018), an officer of Indian Administrative Service, retired as Finance Secretary, Government of Bihar, was one of the closest and distinguished students and associates of Prof. Damodar Thakur.
3. Prof. Jabir Hussain, a distinguished intellectual, former Chairperson of Bihar Legislative Council, and former Professor in English, Magadh University, with whom I had just got connected owing to my write-up on the demise of my father on my blog (and who incidentally had been named as the Chief Editor of the proposed 'wishlist' as mentioned without him being aware of it)
4. Reference to another seminar on 'Education Through Mother-Tongue' organized at the Fair had been made in the preceding lines
5. A copy of the book (*T. S Eliot: An Intensive Study of Selected Poems*) was gifted to Prof. Thakur too, who is reported to have liked the work quite well and sent his congratulations to my father.
6. In fact, all my interactions except the half day spent with him at Patna Book Fair were through letters and, on a few occasions, through telephone.
7. The NBT edition is an abridged version of the title *A Traveller and the Road: The Journey of an Indian Communist* published by Rupa &

Co., New Delhi in 2003. The abridgement of the NBT edition titled *Mohit Sen: An Autobiography,* has been done by Anand Kishore Sahay, and has a foreword by Prof. Bipan Chandra, eminent historian, then Chairman of NBT, and one of the closest friends of Mohit Sen.

8. Sinha, Satchidanand. *Aathwan Din,* (Poetry Collection in Hindi), Radkakrishna Prakashan, New Delhi, 1997
9. Quoted from an unpublished essay provided by Shri S.N. Sinha
10. Prof. G.P. Pradhan (1922–2010), was a veteran socialist leader, reputed educationist, formerly Leader of opposition, Maharashtra Legislative Council and a committed public statesman. Starting out as a Lecturer in English in Pune's Fergusson College where he taught for two decades (1945–65). Strictly speaking, Prof. Pradhan and Prof. Thakur were contemporaries teaching English literature at two parts of the country.
11. First published in Marathi in 1981, the novel depicts primarily the course of life of seven friends who represent seven different discourses in the Nationalist freedom movement in India and post-independence developments. Employing the methods of deconstruction, as it were, the novel not only unfolds the dilemmas, contradictions, dialogue, stories of love, longing, friendships and personal character of the lead players through an omnipresent narrator as well through exchange of letters, entries in diaries etc.

Chapter 17

1. http://lscollege.ac.in/welcome-to-college-website.html
2. "THE EXTRAORDINARY SAGA OF AN ORDINARY PERSON", BADRI NARAYAN SINHA, Nav Rashtra, Patna, Tuesday 2nd March 1965: Phalgun Krishna Paksha 14 Samvat 2021 (Originally in Hindi published under the heading 'Ek Sadharan Manushya Ki Asadharan Kahani'; the present English translation rendered by Shri Adhar Sinha, son of Shri Badri Naryan Sinha and an Indian Administrative Service officer of Andhra Pradesh cadre (1988) with

these notes: "Hyderabad, Wednesday 28th April 2010: Poornima Baisakh 15 Vikram Samvat 2067: Translated from the Hindi original, forty-five years after its publication, by the author's son Shri Adhar Sinha, thanks to his uncle Sachidanand Sinha retrieving this long-lost parchment so as to preserve and propagate this gift to posterity, in order to inspire the generations to come by this saga of extraordinary labour of love for all those peerless values that human life ought to embody indeed."

3. http://www.telegraphindia.com/1110722/jsp/bihar/story_14258673.jsp
4. Dikshit, Surendranath, Presented by: Prof. Nandkishore Prasad Sharma/ *Bihar Ratna Babu Langat Singh: Langat Singh College Ki Vikas Yatra*, Shatabdi Varsh Uphar 1999-2000 (Bihar Gem Babu Langat Singh: The Glorious Journey of Langat Singh College; A Centenary Year Presentation), Published by Tirhut Vikas Vichar Manch, Muzaffarpur, 2000, p.146
5. Sinha, Arun Kumar. *An Introduction to Mark Twain's 'Huckleberry Finn'* (with text), Spectrum Books Pvt. Ltd, New Delhi, 2007, 81-7930-191-5
6. Sinha, Arun Kumar and Kumar Vikram. *T. S. Eliot: An Intensive Study of Selected Poems*, Spectrum Books Pvt. Ltd, New Delhi, (2005, ISBN: 81-7930-173-7
7. Arun Kumar Sinha and Kumar Vikram. *Ramdhari Singh Dinkar: Makers of Indian Literature* (English Translation of Hindi original by Prof. V N Singh), Sahitya Akademi, New Delhi, ISBN 978-81-260-2664-7.
8. "Contributions of ex-principal recalled". *The Times of India*. 30 November, 2011, https://timesofindia.indiatimes.com/city/patna/contributions-of-ex-principal-recalled/articleshow/10926925.cms
9. *Dainik Jagran*, 30 November, 2011, Patna
10. Vikram, Kumar. "Dylan Thomas, his father and my father". http://www.aboutreading.blogspot.in/2012/03/dylan-thomas-his-father-and-my-father.html (under 'Comments' section)
11. ibid (under 'comments' section)

12. Prasad, Anirudh. *University Education, Administration and the Law,* Deep and Deep Publications, New Delhi, 2007, pp. 273-274
13. "Bihar Movement". *Wikipedia,* Wikimedia Foundation, 4 September 2021, https://en.wikipedia.org/wiki/Bihar_Movement
14. *Prabhat Khabar* (A National Hindi Daily), 30 November 2011, Patna.
15. Quoted by Singh, Anuja. *Report Of Seminar On Gandhi: A Leader Of Peace, Harmony, Secularism And Democracy,* Sponsored by University Grants Commission, Kolkata Unit, organized by Department of Political Science, Kamala Rai College, Gopalganj, Bihar, 1st-2nd April 2010 where Prof. Sinha delivered a key-note on Gandhian Values.
16. ibid
17. ibid
18. Sinha, Arun Kumar and Vikram, Kumar. *T. S. Eliot: An Intensive Study of Selected Poems,* Spectrum Books Pvt. Ltd, New Delhi, (2005, p. 3) ISBN: 81-7930-173-7
19. Quoted from the unpublished handwritten manuscript of the novel
20. http://www.speakingtree.in/spiritual-articles/faith-and-rituals/the-strong-brown-god
21. Sinha, Arun Kumar and Kumar Vikram. *Ramdhari Singh Dinkar: Makers of Indian Literature,* (English Translation of Hindi original by Prof. V N Singh): Op. cit, p. 62
22. https://akscentre.wordpress.com/2013/11/28/a-poem-for-bhutto-written-by-aks-on-the-very-next-day-of-bhuttos-execution-on-4th-april-1979/